# IN LIKE A LAMB

—THE STORY OF—
## JOHN BUFFUM

# OUT LIKE A LION

# IN LIKE A LAMB

—THE STORY OF—
## JOHN BUFFUM

# OUT LIKE A LION

## Tom Grimshaw

Tabby House

Manufactured in the United States of America
Library of Congress Number: 93-39119
ISBN: 1-881539-02-4
Cover Design: Lightbourne Images

Library of Congress Cataloging-in-Publication Data
Grimshaw, Tom, 1933-
     In like a lamb—out like a lion : John Buffum, American rally
     driver : his remarkable career and the history of his sport in North
     America / Tom Grimshaw.
       p.   cm.
     Includes bibliographical references (p.297).
     ISBN 1-881539-02-4: $19.95
     1. Buffum, John. 2. Automobile racing drivers—United States—
     -Biography. 3. Automobile rallies—North America—History.
     I. Title.
GV1032.B84R45   1994
796.7'2092—dc20
[B]
                                                              93-39119
                                                                  CIP

Tabby House
Charlotte Harbor, Florida

Dedicated to Mary, who put up with me,
and to Paul, who carries on after me.

—John M. Buffum

# Contents

# Foreword

*I* WAS VERY PLEASED WHEN I was asked to write the foreword for a book covering the career of my friend, John Buffum.

I was John's co-driver on six rallies between 1979 and 1984 and we won five of them; two in the U. S., two in Canada and one in Cyprus. Yet, it's funny that I best remember the one we didn't win—the 1984 Acropolis.

Perhaps we should have been disappointed with our fifth overall [finish] in Greece, but finishing behind a pair each of factory Audis and Lancias, in a Quattro running on street tyres, was a sensational result and far outshone all our victories. John was at his best in Greece. He was very fast right from the start (fourth quickest on the opening stage) and drove an extremely consistent and safe rally in the summertime heat and dust of Greece to beat Timo Salonen by five minutes. (Ironically, Timo is my driver for 1993).

Later that same year he accomplished something no American has done before or since—he won a European Championship Rally. Cyprus is one of the trickiest events on the circuit, very hot, very dusty, and very twisty (we won one stage with an average speed of 28 mph!), but JB never put a wheel wrong. Maybe it was just that the Greek food agreed with

John, although I doubt it since he always carried a jar of peanut butter with him.

Our other rallies together were in North America and there never seemed to be any doubt that we would win them all, such was JB's mastery. There was always someone challenging from the start but come the finish ramp, we were invariably in front.

Rallying with John Buffum was always a lot of fun both inside and outside the car, and I will always look back with happy memories to the times I spent with a very good friend and the times I co-drove for the best rally driver North America has ever produced.

I'm certain everyone will enjoy his book as much as I did.

FRED GALLAGHER
Edinburgh, Scotland
January, 1993

# Preface

**E**VEN THOUGH JOHN BUFFUM'S name is not widely
known to most North American sports fans, I believe a book
detailing his remarkable career is a book that demanded to be
written.

Professional rallying is a major motor sports happening,
rivaling Formula One racing in spectator numbers throughout
the world, with the exception of North America. In the U.S.
and Canada, rallying, in all its various forms, unfortunately has
been and will undoubtedly continue to be, a closet sport.

Despite that fact, it is impossible to ignore the career of an
American driver who currently holds the world record for most
victories in major championship rallies; who has won the U.S.
National PRO Rally Championship eleven times and the combined U.S./Canada North American Rally Cup Championship
nine times; who has broken records on the famed Pikes Peak
Auto Hill Climb; who has been selected three times as a
member of the All-American Race Team by the American Auto
Racing Writers & Broadcasters Association; who is the only
American driver to successfully challenge the foreign stars who
dominate the high powered world of international rallying.

John Buffum's career closely paralleled the roller coaster
rise and fall of professional rallying in North America. In this

book I have attempted to tie the two together, to preserve not only JB's impressive record but also the history of the sport in our small arena.

The title of this book emerged during one of our many hours of taped interviews. John used the expression to describe the cornering technique he preaches to young aspiring rally drivers: "In like a lamb, out like a lion." It seemed an appropriate title since it accurately describes JB's career, from its tentative beginnings in 1969, to its roaring finish in 1987.

I was privileged to be John's co-driver during his final years of active competition. In that time he drove us to several national championships, and more importantly, he became the best friend I will have in this lifetime.

Perhaps this book will help acknowledge my gratitude.

TOM GRIMSHAW
Rotonda West, Florida
August, 1993

# Acknowledgments

I T IS VIRTUALLY IMPOSSIBLE to write a biographical book of any length without relying on the experiences and recollections of others. It is also unwise to ignore assistance and support when it is kindly offered. Realizing that few men build lasting structures alone, I wish to acknowledge the following contributions: To the many authors and journalists whose work I used for reference and often quoted— because they wrote so well I would not dare attempt to do better—Tim Cline, Michael Jordan, Jay Lamm, Martin Holmes, John Watson, David Abrahamson, Cameron Warren, Jean Calvin and Sam Moses.

To fellow competitors who permitted us to mine their memories and who often jogged our own—Gene Henderson, Virginia Reese, Ken Adams, Robin Edwardes and John Grimshaw.

To John Buffum's mother, Emily—who graciously shared her memories and her home for several months; whose letters and cards from around the world always prompted me to begin again; who cooks a great breakfast and provides a fine selection of wines.

To John's wife, Mary—whose continuous good humor and long lasting personal friendship is only matched by her unflagging support of this project—and for her patience in teaching me how to properly devour an entire lobster.

And finally to all those I left standing in the woods—those who I have omitted in error. Your absence is not intentional.

TOM GRIMSHAW
1993

# PART ONE

*1969 Monte Carlo Rallye XXXVIII. Lt. John Buffum and Stephen (Yogi) Behr on the start ramp in the No. 85 Porsche 911-T.*

# 1

# Monte Carlo 1969
## The Beginning—In Like A Lamb

$T$HE 1969 MONTE CARLO RALLYE was by far the most prestigious performance rally of its time. The thirty-eighth presentation of the "Monte" was the opening round of the European Rally Championship season and attracted most of the premier factory teams of the day.

Among the 224 drivers included in the starting line-up were many names familiar to current day enthusiasts: Hannu Mikkola, Vic Elford, Pat Moss Carlsson, Bjorn Waldegaard, Harry Kallstrom, Rauno Aaltonen, Tony Fall, Timo Makinen, Simo Lampinen, and many others. Hidden somewhere in that impressive list was the name of a totally unknown twenty-five-year-old American amateur—U.S. Army Lieutenant John M. Buffum, driving a privately-entered red and black Porsche 911T with the letters "USA" outlined in adhesive tape on the roof.

Nobody paid much attention to Lt. Buffum and rightly so. He had never before competed in a major rally. Also, in 1969 there were no American drivers known to the international rally community. However, the official program did mention in passing that John Buffum was the sole entry from the United States among the twenty-two countries represented.

The 2,250 mile Monte Carlo Rallye began January 17 in eight different cities: Athens, Rheims, Frankfort, London, Monte Carlo, Lisbon, Warsaw and Oslo. Lt. Buffum, on leave from his army post in Germany, started as Car 85. There were no seeding rules for drivers in those days and the number merely designated a start location of Frankfort, Germany.

Buffum's co-driver was Stephen (Yogi) Behr, a thirty-year-old former U.S. Air Force captain from Greenwich, Connecticut, who was then working in Germany as a Porsche salesman. Yogi Behr had never competed in a rally!

Their service crew consisted of Buffum's wife, Vicki, and two army buddies: Platoon Sgt. Frank Wood and Spec. 5 James (Salty) Sottolano. Midway through the rally, Wood and Sottolano had to leave on field maneuvers.

The Associated Press issued daily reports on the 1969 Monte Carlo Rallye and the *New York Times* and *Stars and Stripes* carried extensive coverage of the famous event:

*January 19—Saint Claude, France*
"American John Buffum of Wallingford, Connecticut is among the early leaders of The Monte Carlo Rallye. Driving and calculating with slide-rule precision, Buffum's Porsche shot along the snow packed twisty mountain roads to arrive today at this checkpoint with no penalty points." (Associated Press, *New York Times*)

*January 21—Monaco*
"Rauno Aaltonen of Finland and Henry Liddon of Britain, who won the 1967 Monte Carlo Auto Rallye, abandoned this year's event tonight after their Lancia slammed into the side of a mountain. Lieut. John Buffum was doing well enough in the Alpine Stages to qualify for the final stages." *(Stars and Stripes)*

*January 22—Monte Carlo*

"After the first stage of the 888-mile Alpine Loop, Hannu Mikkola of Finland, with co-driver Jim Porter of Britain, lead the XXXVIII Rallye Monte Carlo in a Ford Escort. Bjorn Waldegaard, Sweden, is second in a Porsche." (AP, *NYT*)

*January 23—Monte Carlo*

"Fantastically severe weather conditions in the French Alps cut the final stage of The Monte Carlo Rallye to only 54 cars. Ice and snow in the run from Monaco to Vals-les-Bains, Chambery, Digne and back to Monaco brought on numerous crashes.

"Tony Fall and John Davenport of Britain crashed 200 feet down a canyon Tuesday night in their Lancia. They were miraculously unhurt.

"Lt. John Buffum's Porsche is 18th, although it was dented on one side when it slid off the road." (AP, *NYT*)

*January 24—Monte Carlo*

"A Swedish pair, competing in only their second Monte Carlo Rallye—Bjorn Waldegaard and Lars Helmer–gave the Stuttgart Porsche factory a convincing victory in the annual Monte Carlo classic. Lt. John M. Buffum of Wallingford, Conn. and Stephen Behr of Greenwich, Conn. finished twelfth in a Porsche. It was the first Monte Carlo Rallye for both."*(Stars and Stripes)*

Headlines announced:

"U.S. SOLDIER CAPTURES 12TH IN FAMED MONTE CARLO RALLYE" (*New York Times*)

"BUFFUM 12TH IN MONTE CARLO, HIGHEST EVER BY AN AMERICAN" (*Stars and Stripes*)

"BUFFUM SAYS: DREAM COME TRUE" (*Stars and Stripes*)

And the finale in *Stars and Stripes*:

*January 25–Monte Carlo* (Photo Caption)

"First Lieutenant John Buffum was clad in his army dress blues, his driving partner, Stephen Behr, wore a tuxedo and Buffum's vivacious wife, Vicki, appeared in sparkling humor in a new gown. The three happy young Americans were on their way to Prince Ranier's gala dinner for Monte Carlo competitors."

**B**jorn Waldegaard repeated his victory the following year. He also won the first world championship for drivers in 1979 and most recently took first overall in the 1990 Safari Rally, driving for Toyota Team Europe.

The 1969 Monte Carlo Rallye was one of Waldegaard's earliest victories in a major international rally but it was not a surprising upset. After all, he was a Porsche factory driver, a professional paid to win.

John Buffum followed his astounding Monte Carlo performance with three more outstanding drives during his remaining months in Germany. He and Behr finished tenth overall, first in class, and first amateur team on the 1,700 kilometer Lyon-Charbonnieres-Stuttgart-Solitude Rally and joined up again to take another class win at the six-hundred kilometer Trifels Rally.

Vicki Buffum co-drove for her husband on the French Criterium Neige et Glace Rally. Their Porsche finished fifteenth overall and third in class.

Still, we can only imagine the dinner conversation back in 1969 when the final results of the XXXVIII Monte Carlo Rallye were announced at Prince Ranier's gala dinner: "WHO THE HELL IS JOHN BUFFUM?"

*1.1 "Yogi" Behr (L) and John Buffum (R) posing with the No. 85
Porsche 911-T (with "USA" marked on the roof by adhesive tape)
before the start of the 1969 Monte Carlo Rallye.*

**JB:** **"**I lucked out when I entered the army in 1967
because I had a degree in mathematics and they put me in the
Corps of Engineers at a time when they were making cooks out
of heart surgeons.

I took my officer's training at Fort Belvoir, Virginia and
was shipped to Germany for a year and a half before returning
home to be discharged as a first lieutenant. We built Bailey
Bridges in Germany . . . actually we transported them and the
grunts (army infantrymen) erected them. Basically, we were
technical supervision.

Soon after our daughter, Courtney, was born, Vicki brought
her to Germany and we lived off base for most of my overseas
duty.

Back then the Monte Carlo Rallye was the most important
international rally in the world—nothing else compared to it,

*1.2 JB sliding the Porsche through an icy turn on an alpine stage of the 1969 Monte Carlo Rallye. (Photo: Attualfoto)*

not even the African Safari. Because of its international stature it had already attracted several American manufacturers. Scott Harvey and Gene Henderson, who both became U.S. national driving champions some years later, ran the 1964 Monte together in a Chrysler Valiant, but they finished back in eightieth overall and fifth in class. As Henderson says, 'We didn't exactly terrorize 'em over there.'

Ford entered a team of Falcons in '63 and '64 but they also did not do well and one of their drivers was killed when his car went off the road during pacenoting in the Alps. Americans just couldn't compete in the international arenas back then.

In 1968 I forged Harry Handley's signature to a letter and applied to The Monte organizers for press credentials, which I received. Harry was the rally director of the Sports Car Club of America (SCCA) at that time.

So I took some leave and Vicki and I followed Vic Elford's factory Porsche throughout the rally. I think it was Vicki's blond hair that attracted their attention and allowed us to tag along with the Porsche team. They looked at her and said, 'Oh yeah, this guy's okay.'

Elford won The Monte that year and I got to know a lot of the people at Porsche. I still hear from Vic every few years and he visited us a couple of times. A few years ago he called looking for a job in the automotive business but I wasn't able to help him with that.

I was stationed about five miles from the Porsche factory in Germany and when I called them up some time after the rally they remembered me (or Vicki) and we arranged to buy one of their practice cars. I did nineteen events in Europe between March '68 and April '69. Most of them were fast TSD rallies. Sometimes I drove but often I enjoyed navigating using a 'Zeitabelle' (German timetables), and large scale maps.

We didn't have service crews in those days but the Porsche factory had its own service department and they took care of our car between rallies. The mechanics were always sneaking some exotic performance part into my car but management always made us return it . . . when they caught us.

I never won a rally in Germany back then but we got a few gold medals for finishing in the top 10 percent of our class and a couple of cups, but no overall wins.

One night I had barracks duty and sent one of my guys out for some drinks. I gave him the keys to the Porsche and he ran it off the road and landed under a barn, which collapsed. Both the barn and the car were totaled. We bought a second Porsche 911T from Helmut Klocke who did German National Championship rallies and that's the same car we ran on the 1969 Monte Carlo Rallye and later brought back to the U.S.

I was originally supposed to run the '69 Monte with Jurgen Barth from the Porsche factory but at the last minute he couldn't make it so I teamed up with an American I hardly

23

knew, Steven Behr. Jurgen went on to win the LeMans 24 Hour Race and remains a very good friend today. His father, Edgar Barth, was hill-climbing champion of Europe three times and won the famous Targa Florio race.

Vic Elford and his co-driver, David Stone, had taught me how to do pacenotes so I'd take a three day pass, blow down to the course Thursday night, practice three days, and return to base on Sunday. The pacenoting was much like we do today but not so complicated—not so many degrees of turns as we now use.

Then just before the start of The Monte I tripped and fell down a flight of stairs. I also had laryngitis so I was not in very good shape to be running my very first world class rally.

We started in Frankfort, did a long run across northern France, then down the west side, across the bottom of France and met everybody at Digne. From there the whole rally drove to Monte Carlo. The first section was thirty-six straight hours and we finished it with no penalty points—and no sleep.

In Monte Carlo we got a twelve hour rest then did a twenty-four hour, nineteen-stage loop from Monaco to Vals-les-Bains to Chambery, Switzerland, then returned to Monaco. The final section was a twelve-hour, eleven-stage Alpine loop from Monaco and back to the finish.

Halfway through the final night Yogi and I were both falling asleep on the road and a BMW 2002TI from Switzerland beat us for first amateur team. I think we could have beaten them if we hadn't been so tired.

During the rally we often switched seats because Yogi had done some asphalt racing and I was pretty good in the ice and snow. We only had three sets of tires for the entire rally. The tires and a few gas cans were our total service setup.

The army hadn't known where I'd gone when I took a seven day leave to run The Monte but we got a lot of coverage in *Stars and Stripes* and when I returned to my base they'd put

24

up a huge banner reading, 'WELCOME BACK 12TH.' That was really great.

I met Bjorn Waldegaard when he won the 1969 Monte

*1.3 Gene Henderson (driving) and Scott Harvey wind their way through the Alps in a factory-sponsored Chrysler Valiant on the 1964 Monte Carlo Rallye.*

Carlo Rallye and I still have a picture of us together back then, although I didn't know him very well at that time. I was just another guy.**"**

The month following Buffum's surprising performance on The Monte Carlo Rallye he received a congratulatory letter from the Sports Car Club of America together with a batch of Associated Press news clippings. The letter was signed by rally director, Harry Handley.

At the finish of the 1969 Monte Carlo Rallye a reporter asked Lt. Buffum if he had any plans to continue rallying when he returned to the United States in May.

John answered, "No, I don't have any plans in that direction."

# 2
## Brief History of Rallying
### Let The Games Begin

*H*ERODOTUS IS QUOTED as saying in 484 B.C., "Very few things happen at the right time and the rest do not happen at all. The conscientious historian will correct these defects."

Certainly he was referring to the history of motor sports and more specifically, to the history of rallying.

Most historians agree motor sports began at 8:00 A.M. the morning of July 22, 1894 when twenty-two cars began the Paris-Rouen Reliability Test Run organized by *Petit Journal* magazine. It is interesting to note both "racing" and "rallying" publicists often claim this event as the birth of their respective forms of madness.

Historians correcting defects?

Regardless, rallies were originally called "trials." The first organized rally was England's 1,000 Miles Trial, held in 1900. Sixty-five cars ran a tour from London to several major cities such as Bristol, Manchester, Edinburgh and Leeds. Fifty-one finishers returned to London.

Rallying, which began as a competition designed for amateurs interested in pleasure use of their automobiles, took a more serious turn in 1907 with the 7,500 mile Peking-Paris Rally.

That event came about when Prince Scipione Burghese challenged several of his acquaintances to a motor car competition. Five teams, including the prince's, took up the gauntlet. The Parisian daily, *Le Matin,* stepped forth as sponsor and the competition began June 10, 1907.

Two months later, on August 10, the prince, accompanied by his chauffeur, Ettore, and Luigi Barzini, were the only team to finish in Paris. The prince (or his chauffeur) drove a 40 hp Itala.

There is some disagreement about the longest rally ever held. Some opt for the New York to Paris run of 1908. This bit of insanity ran through Alaska and Siberia, over 22,000 miles in 169 days. Teams had to build their own bridges and roads in remote areas—but, they got extra credit for doing so.

*2.1 The 1907 Thomas Flyer that won the 1908 New York to Paris Race (rally?)—still alive and well and competing on the 1986 Great American Race.*

The New York to Paris Race was won by a Thomas Flyer which finished twenty-six days in front of the second place car!

Purists claim the New York to Paris event was a "race" not a "rally." They claim the Singapore Airlines sponsored London-Sydney Rally was the longest in history. That event began August 13, 1977 in Covent Garden of Greater London and finished September 28 at the Sydney, Australia, Opera House. It passed through seventeen countries and covered 19,329 miles.

Andrew Cowan teamed with Colin Malkin and Michael Broad to win in a Mercedes 280E.

The *Guinness Book of World Records* lists the London-Sydney Rally as the longest in history and who is to argue with that long established authority?

The American Automobile Association sponsored what might have been the first American rally. In 1904 the AAA presented a run from New York City to the World's Fair in St. Louis.

The following year, Charles Jasper Glidden, one of the earliest American sports car enthusiasts, gave a $2,000 trophy to the AAA for what then became "The Glidden Tour." It ran from New York City through the New England states until 1913 when AAA lost interest.

Rallying in the U.S. and Canada began to grow in popularity following World War II. Returning servicemen told wild tales of rally escapades in Europe where the sport had grown steadily since the early 1900s (the Monte Carlo Rallye began in 1911).

At that same time foreign automobile imports began arriving on our eastern shores in ever increasing numbers. Since most American mechanics, because of lack of expertise or the proper tools, could not, or would not, work on foreign sports cars, owners shared their common woes with the formation of sports car clubs. Most of those early organizations

29

were "marque" clubs, such as The Volkswagen Club of America, where drivers of like makes could trade secrets to keep their new toys running.

It wasn't long before members of sports car clubs began organizing competitions as diversions for their members. Most went racing. A few—those who could not afford weekly repairs to their cars—organized tours.

Tours soon evolved into competitive rallies—a game people played with their cars—and the game began to move across the U.S. and Canada.

Rallying was like any other game. If you let enough people play it over a period of time you will soon have to devise a method of declaring a winner. So organizers began to customize their events. They developed little "gimmicks" to fool competitors and separate the winners from the losers.

For instance, a route book instruction might read: "Begin average speed of 42 mph at the next stop sign, while assuming at the same time a car, fifty-one miles away, has begun traveling towards you at 50 mph. When you meet the car—turn left on a side road."

This "Phantom Car Problem" was a favorite gimmick of rally-masters many years ago.

A small group of enthusiasts did not have the patience required for the mind-baffling games and precise timing and measurements required in Time-Speed-Distance (TSD) rallying. To quote the late American race and rally driver, Jon Woodner, they just wanted to be involved "with real people, in real cars, going real fast down real roads."

Two events in the fifties pandered to this small group.

The first was The Great American Mountain Rally in 1953. It was organized by the Motorsports Club of America and received a calendar listing from the Federation International de L'Automobile (FIA), a Paris-based group of international representatives who regulate motor sports throughout the world.

The GAMR, held on Thanksgiving weekend, started and finished in Poughkeepsie, New York, and ran as far north as New Canaan, Vermont. Its rules were fairly simple: no one was to exceed forty miles per hour. Those who did received a four-minute penalty for every early arrival minute.

The three-day rally was won by Stew Blodget in an MG with 3,898 points. Walter Cronkite was listed among the also-rans.

The following year Rootes Motors of England entered two Sunbeams in the Great American Mountain Rally. Stirling Moss, a Formula One racing legend, teamed with an American navigator, Ron Russell, in one car while Shiela VanDamm and Anne Hall ran the other.

An Oldsmobile won the rally.

In 1955, in an attempt to emulate the Monte Carlo format, the GAMR started in eleven different U.S. cities, but it never received much recognition in Europe and was finally canceled in 1957.

The second major happening, which delighted the small but enthusiastic go-fast crowd, was the Press On Regardless Rally in Michigan.

The POR began in 1949 as a tour of western Michigan. It started and finished at Greenfield Village in Dearborn. Bill Wood, nephew of the late powerboat champion/industrialist, Gar Wood, supposedly gave the event its title.

"The phrase 'press on regardless' is in a quote from Winston Churchill," Wood explained.

Why Winston Churchill?

"Because we all drove British sports cars back then."

Recently a second version explaining the POR title surfaced through the recollections of Harold Lance, a member of the original organizing group. "Bill Wood, first regional executive of the Detroit Region SCCA, arrived while we were discussing a name for our big rally—something like Michigan Overnight Rally, I think—anyway, Bill inquired if we had yet named this 'press on regardless' thing, and that was it!"

By the early sixties the POR had become an ass-busting endurance bash through the forest trails of Michigan's Lower Peninsula.

It retained its pseudo-legal status as a public road rally by continuing the traditional TSD format. The difference between it and other TSD rallies of the time was that the POR, beginning in 1961 under the co-chairmanship of Scott Harvey and Gene Henderson, covered 1,000 miles over twenty-four non-stop hours and required average speeds (within legal limits) that could not be maintained on the small, twisty forest trails of Michigan. Cable winches, bull-bags and other deditching equipment were commonplace.

In other words, the fastest *surviving* driver won the rally.

During the mid-sixties many other "underground" fast TSD rallies, such as The Dawnbuster, The Moonlight Monte, and Tri-State 24 Hour Rally began to appear with increased regularity.

Similarly in Canada, events such as the Canadian Winter Rally and Rallye des Neiges were run under the basic TSD format while actually catering to the drivers "need for speed."

The general format for most of those early "pro-rally" events included a mixture of fast and leisurely-paced transits on major roads leading to very brisk average speed sections on little-traveled roads in remote areas. Hidden checkpoints were located in the fast average speed sections.

Timing and scoring were originally based on the whole-minute concept. A team would receive a zero penalty if they arrived at a check point any time within the correct arrival minute, that is, no more than thirty seconds early or late. As performances improved, this system resulted in many ties and timing was soon changed to the exact second to separate the top teams.

The primary challenge on those early high speed TSD events was to stay on time, but some rallies, especially in Canada, also included a few navigational problems to spice up the game. Tricks, such as cumulative mileage turns listed in scrambled order, were often employed to test the navigator's ability to keep his driver on course as well as on time.

Concurrent with the emergence of speed events in North America, European rallying had also been changing. Rallies were beginning to stress speed and endurance, but the roads of Europe had become crowded as more and more people gained access to inexpensive automobiles. High speed rallying on open roads had become too dangerous, both for the public and the competitors.

Rallying, if it were to continue, had to adapt to changing times . . . and so it did, with the introduction of "closed stages."

*2.2 Rallying in the good old days of two-wheel-drive. A co-driver lends his weight to improve rear wheel traction on the 1976 African Safari Rally. Cars were often fitted with foot plates and hand holds for just this purpose. (Photo: Colin Taylor Productions)*

# 3
## Closing Public Roads
### Trials, Selectives and Stages

*T* HE TRANSITION FROM Time-Speed-Distance rallying to the current format of "Closed Stages" was not immediate. It began with the introduction, within the traditional TSD format, of increased average speeds, thereby placing more emphasis on driving skills and vehicle endurance and less on navigational and mathematical proficiency. The challenge was shifting from the navigator to the driver.

Bowing to public pressure, organizers began to introduce "selectives" (sometimes called "trials") into their events.

Selectives were portions of a rally course where teams were required to drive as quickly as possible. Most selectives were held on race tracks or on lightly traveled roads, such as private roads or on army bases, etc. Organizers were usually given permission to "control" traffic, but were not allowed to officially close the road to the public. Scoring was based on elapsed time rather than matching an average speed to the exact second—the shorter the elapsed time the lower the score (or penalty).

Selectives became very popular in North America with the advent of the Shell Trans-Canada 4000 Rally in 1961, jointly sponsored by the British Columbia International Trade Fair and the Shell Oil Company. The original event began in Montreal and finished seven days later in Vancouver. In later years the coast-to-coast route was reversed.

The Shell coast-to-coast rallies were very demanding as teams were challenged by the "cresty" roads of Quebec, the rocks of Northern Ontario, the slippery mud of Manitoba, the sticky "gumbo" of Saskatchewan, and the mountain snows and high elevations of British Columbia—and all were open to public travel. Most of the starting fields did not finish the long ordeal. The Shell, at that time, was the most important rally in North America. In 1964 the World Rally Championship for Makes (manufacturers) nominated five events for their calendar: The East African Safari (Africa), The RAC Rally (England), Rally of the Midnight Sun (Finland), Marathon de la Route (Southern Europe), and the Shell 4000 Trans-Canada Rally.

In keeping with the Shell's world championship status it was necessary to add several high speed sections (stages) that were totally closed to public travel during the passage of the rally. Jim Gunn, the event coordinator, recruited Peter Bone, a Canadian race and rally driver with European stage-rally experience, to organize these new segments.

New safety regulations were introduced, including helmets, full roll bars and complete racing harnesses. The new course format included North America's first closed stage— The Cascades Road—a little used public road (it had been by-passed by a new paved highway) from Lake Christina to Rossland, B.C.

The very twisty dirt road covered thirty-three miles over two mountain passes with many unguarded hairpin turns and sheer drops of 2,000 feet or more.

Competitors sitting at the start line of The Cascades Stage were greeted by a large sign warning that the gravel road they were about to race through, in the dark, at frightening speeds and dangerous elevations, "was no longer maintained for public use."

The Shells attracted the likes of Paddy Hopkirk, disqualified one year for using an extra oil cooler; Rosemary Smith, an

Irish clothes designer and professional rally driver who later appeared on the television show "What's My Line?" and England's premier driver, Roger Clark, who won the event in 1967, driving a Lotus Cortina for Ford Canada.

One year a group of Canadian physicians used The Shell to study the effects of stress and sleeplessness on competitors.

An interesting result seemed to indicate that drivers' pulse rates increased radically during high speed sections, while co-drivers' pulse rates either remained constant or actually slowed down. No one ever hypothesized whether this meant drivers were more aware of the dangers or if co-drivers were simply too busy (and perhaps too trusting) to recognize their peril.

The rally was cancelled in 1969 when Shell Oil withdrew its sponsorship. The final event in 1968 was won by Americans Scott Harvey and Ralph Beckman in a Plymouth Barracuda.

In 1968 Canadians Robin Edwardes, a very experienced navigator, and Klauss Ross, a former rally driving champion and two-time winner of the Shell 4000, wrote new rules and timing procedures, finally introducing high speed selectives to Canadian rallies at the national level.

Thirty-one selectives were included in the 1968, 750-mile Dow Quebec National Rally and a new era of high speed rallying began in North America.

That same year organizers of Michigan's Press On Regardless Rally finally set aside their reluctance to approach authorities with a request to close public roads, and a formal stage (Connor's Flats) was included in the Sports Car Club of America National Championship TSD event.

David Kuehne and David Cady from Rochester, New York were the winners of the first official closed stage in the U.S. They drove a Saab 96 through the 6.33 miles of Connor's Flats in eight minutes and twenty-seven seconds to beat Gene Henderson and Wayne Zitkus' Plymouth Barracuda by *one* second.

Connor's Flats was only a very small segment in a twenty-four hour 1,000 mile course, but it proved that permission could be obtained to close public roads in North America just as in other parts of the rally world.

While North America was slow to adopt the selective/stage format, Europe had already committed totally to "closed stages."

A "stage" rally course is made up of short races over roads closed to public travel during passage of the event. The closed roads (special stages) are connected by public road "transits" traversed at legal speeds. The fastest accumulative times over the closed stage roads determines the winner of the event.

The famed RAC International Rally in England introduced its first closed stage in 1960. It was a short sprint across Scottish moorland at Monument Hill. Eric Carlsson's little 2-stroke Saab bashed its way to an easy victory and began the onslaught on the forest roads of England. The following year the RAC changed to an all-stage format.

Today's World Rally Championship Series includes stage rallies in many countries on several continents. Professional rallying has become very big business. Spectators number in the millions and their numbers continue to grow each year because many special stages are run on public roads near large population centers, which in turn generates increased media attention. Drivers and co-drivers (navigators) are highly paid professionals and manufacturers budget millions of dollars to showcase their products.

Throughout the world professional rallying rivals Formula One racing over all other forms of motor sport activity—except in North America.

In the U.S. and Canada, rallying in the late sixties and early seventies continued to be an amateur sport. There were no factory-sponsored teams competing for a national championship consisting of stage rallies. National championships

38

continued to be based on the traditional Time-Speed-Distance format.

After its single stage experiment in 1968, the POR expanded to four closed stages in 1969 (Connor's Flats, Chippewa River, Downey Mann Truck Trail, and Tin Shanty Road) and thirty in 1970 when it was granted FIA international calendar status.

Those first stages were called "M" Sections. No one can remember if the "M" stood for "Michigan," "Mayhem," or "Murder."

Often times the public roads used as stages were so infrequently traveled they were little more than grass covered trails.

Indeed one year the event organizer used a road that was so obscure he had to place small wooden stakes in several places to define the correct route. When he explained their use to a companion during a pre-check of the course, the companion remarked, "They're swell!" From that moment forward the small course markers were known as "swell stakes."

Despite the transition to high speed rallying in the U.S. there was no cohesive series of performance rallies until 1970 when the MG Car Club of Cleveland, Ohio, organized the MONY Series which included seven events in Michigan, Ohio, and New York counting towards an overall championship. Some of the rallies were a combination of TSD and selectives, others were just very fast TSD events.

The initial MONY driving champion was Dick Zwitzer of Rochester, New York. Zwitzer continued to compete for several years but retired before an official national championship of stage rallies was established.

The MONY Series was the forerunner of the SCCA National PRO Rally Championship Series and was disbanded in 1974 because most of its events were also included on the SCCA National Championship circuit.

While most high speed rally activity in the sixties was centered in the eastern portion of the U.S., the west coast soon followed suit. A loose federation of California clubs (called The Four Cylinder Clubs) organized several speed events on paved roads. While average speeds were still used, they were set so high as to be impossible to maintain and crashes were not infrequent.

Fiats and Alfas were the favored rides because of their advantageous power to weight ratios.

A single paved "stage" was included in the 1970 Nor'wester Rally in Washington state as the Northwest also got into step with the rest of the country.

The transition to full stage rallying on the west coast took place in April, 1972 when Ken Adams, a Californian rallyist with many years experience in the U.S. and Mexico, introduced the La Jornada Trabajosa Rally.

From that date forward, thinly-disguised, high-speed TSD events run on glass-smooth roads quickly faded from the west coast scene.

In 1973 the Sports Car Club of America, acknowledging the pressure from a small group of rally members, but more importantly, noting the financial success of stage rallying in the rest of the world, established the National PRO Rally Championship Series which continues today.

Separate national championship series for TSD rallies and stage rallies still exist in the U.S., while Canada dropped TSD rallies as a national series and replaced it with an all-stage format in 1973.

The first SCCA National PRO Rally Driving Champion was Scott Harvey, a Chrysler engineer from Michigan who had dominated U.S. rallying for many years. The following year, the title went to Gene Henderson, a police officer from Dearborn, Michigan who had shared driving duties with Harvey on the 1964 Monte Carlo Rallye.

40

It is interesting to note that Henderson won his championship in a four-wheel-drive Jeep Cherokee, years before 4WD began to dominate rallying throughout the world. His surprising success in a vehicle so large and cumbersome it was named "Moby Dick," immediately drew negative reactions against the "unfair advantage of 4WD trucks."

As a result of the uproar, the FIA banned four-wheel-drive vehicles from international rally competition throughout the seventies. However, they were still permitted in the national events of North America.

In 1973 the POR was included in the FIA World Championships for Makes and was being considered as a full world championship event for both makes and drivers in 1974. Two Canadians, Walter Boyce and Doug Woods, won the event in a Toyota Corolla and even today remain the only North American team to ever win a world championship rally.

In 1974, the FIA finally acknowledged stage rallying in North America and placed the Press On Regardless (U.S.) and Rideau Lakes (Canada) on its calendar of the World Championship for Rallies.

North American rallyists were ecstatic. Finally they could test their abilities against the best in the world. Big time professional rallying was coming to America. Unfortunately, the long anticipated event turned into an embarrassing fiasco.

Foreign rally drivers were not used to observing strict speed limits during transits on public roads between race stages. They were welcomed in most countries by throngs of spectators who cheered as police waved them through crowded intersections in large cities and small villages. Not so in America.

Sandro Munari, an Italian driver who had won the famed Monte Carlo Rallye four times, and was the 1973 European

41

*3.1 Gene Henderson and Ken Pogue bashing their way to victory in the 4-wheel-drive "Moby Dick" (Jeep Cherokee) on the 1972 POR in Michigan.*

Rally Champion, drove his Lancia Stratos through Feltch, a small Michigan town, at speeds nearing 100 mph—at dusk on Halloween Night! The local sheriff gave chase and when he failed to catch the Stratos on the transit he proceeded down the following closed stage. Finally, in frustration, he returned to the stage start-line placed his car across the road, laid a shotgun on the hood and stopped the rally.

Event organizers panicked. Since the stage was open for competition and some cars had already raced through it, the international rules of *force majeure* indicated the majority of the field—those turned back by the irate and well-armed sheriff—be declared non-finishers with over half of the rally still to be run.

Team managers screamed at the rally chairman in several languages, threatened to sue, quoted international rally rules,

*3.2 Sandro Munari, winner of the 1977 Monte Carlo Rallye, in the same type of Lancia Stratos that caused the problems on the 1974 POR world championship rally in Michigan. (Photo: Colin Taylor Productions)*

and generally terrorized the novice officials while competitors sat and waited for a decision.

Three hours passed before the organizers finally decided to restart the entire field and let the FIA sort out the mess back in Paris.

Some months later, after the FIA reviewed all the resulting protests, Jean-Luc Therier was declared the winner in a Renault 17 Gordini, followed by Markku Alen in a Fiat Abarth 124.

The POR was removed from the FIA calendar and world championship rallying was not to return to America for another ten years.

In 1975 John Buffum, the young American soldier who startled the international rally world with his unprecedented twelfth-place finish on the 1969 Monte Carlo Rallye, became the National PRO Rally Driving Champion of the United States.

He was to repeat as national champion ten more times before his retirement from active competition at the close of the '87 season. He also added nine North American Rally Cup Championships (a combined U.S./Canada stage rally series) to his list of major titles.

And, to cap his outstanding career, in 1987 John Buffum became the world record holder for most overall victories in major championship stage rallies!

If, as Andy Warhol once proclaimed, we are famous for only fifteen minutes, it must be said that John Buffum used every second of his alloted time to the fullest.

But back in the early seventies, when professional rallying was about to emerge in North America as a viable form of motor sport, we were just beginning to learn the answer to the question, "Who the hell is John Buffum?"

# 4
# Fun on a Saturday Night
## Growing Up In Switzerland

**W**HAT FACTORS DETERMINE that one individual will rise above the rest in their chosen field of endeavor? Are great athletes born to greatness or are they born to be athletes and trained to greatness? Is it an accident of timing, being born in the right place at the right time? Is it the cumulative result of childhood influences or a fortunate combination of ability, desire and opportunity?

Perhaps it is all of these things and more. Perhaps it is some "extra" quality we do not quite fathom.

Perhaps it is a genetic gift.

John Buffum's mother, Emily, recalls, "John's father [John Harold Buffum, Jr.] always loved speed. He was a fighter pilot and kept a motorboat down on Long Island Sound, and he owned a motorcycle and a little green Terraplane.

"He also was a bit of a maverick and once buzzed the Wallingford Country Club in his airplane, and was severely reprimanded for it. He'd just won the amateur golf tournament at that same club.

"It seemed he was always doing something he shouldn't be doing, like telling off his commanding officer or some other outrageous act.

"If Buff were alive today, he and John would probably be rallying together and arguing about who would drive and who would navigate."

When the Japanese bombed Pearl Harbor on December 7, 1941, John Harold Buffum, Jr. was already a lieutenant in the U.S. Army Air Force. Shortly after the attack he was posted to the Panama Canal Zone to train fighter pilots against an expected invasion.

A few months later, Emily Merwin of Wallingford, Connecticut, joined Lt. Buffum in Panama and the two were married there in the Congregational church.

In April, 1943, Captain Buffum died in a training accident over the Pacific, when his airplane was hit by another as it emerged from a cloud formation. He was twenty-seven years old and had been married to Emily for two years.

Their son, John Merwin Buffum, was born October 4, 1943 in New Haven, Connecticut.

Emily tells of her son's childhood:

"My father passed away just before I brought Buff home to be buried in Wallingford, so my mother and I moved into an old house and raised young John together.

"He was always a quiet child, perhaps because he lived with two women, and couldn't get a word in edgewise. He could always do whatever he wanted to do, although he never tried awfully hard unless something really interested him, like geography (his favorite school subject), or hockey, or skiing.

"When John was five years old, we began taking him on vacations to New Hampshire where he learned to ski. We stayed in a cottage that had flying bats in it and my mother would get up at night, put on her bathing cap, take her tennis racket, and whop 'em.

"I guess I was a pretty strict mother. I hate whiners and sissies.

46

"We lived close to Choate Boys School in Wallingford. Joe and Jack Kennedy had gone to Choate and I worked there for a short time until I opened my own secretarial service. Since I knew the people and it wasn't very expensive in those days we entered John in the eighth grade and he graduated from Choate.

"John's paternal grandfather passed away and left him $10,000 for his education. It came at a fortunate time because I was worried about him spending too much time at home with two women.

"One night I was reading *The Saturday Evening Post* and noticed an article about American boys going to school in Switzerland where they could play hockey–which John loved to do–learn French, ski, and still get a very good education. I decided to send him to Switzerland to repeat his junior high school year.

"When he was sixteen my mother and I delivered him to Lycee Jaccard, a small prep school on the edge of Lake Geneva. He'd never been away from home and emotionally he was more like a thirteen-year-old than a sixteen-year-old. He was scared and homesick but he spent nine months in Switzerland before returning home to complete his final year at Choate.

"David Niven's son, Jamie, was his roommate for a term. John wrote that he'd met David Niven and "he seemed just like an ordinary guy."

"John and a classmate traveled all over Europe, visiting most of the major cities before he sailed home from England. We picked him up in New York. He only had a single dime left in his pocket.

"Switzerland turned out to be one of the wisest decisions I've ever made. My son left home as a boy and returned a young man."

4.1 John Buffum, 1961, captain of the Lycee Jaccard hockey team; 4.2 competing in a year-end ski race between prep schools in Zweisimmen, Switzerland.

After graduating from Choate, John applied to Harvard, Middlebury and Colby, and was accepted at all three schools. He chose Middlebury "because I felt I'd get lost at Harvard and wanted to know the people I was going to be with."

He entered Middlebury (Vermont) College in 1962 and never went home again.

In his sophomore and junior years at Middlebury he was a disc jockey playing rock and roll music on a college station, which later became public station WRMC. His first stint began at 6:00 A.M. when the station first came on the air and he'd blast everyone awake with "Reveille Rock." Later he got a top ten show from nine to ten in the evening and "got to talk to a lot of girls calling in their requests."

(Many years later John Buffum's disc jockey experience earned him the title of "uncrowned king of music trivia." After hearing just a few opening bars he could name the tune, the year it was released, and the performing artists—much to the disgust of his companions on very long rallies where CB radio trivia contests are the popular pastime.)

**JB:** "I never cared much for cars when I was growing up. Probably because I didn't go out much and then at Middlebury, freshmen weren't allowed to have cars.

When I became a sophomore I used the remaining money I'd received from my grandfather and bought a new '64 Corvair Monza Spyder for $2,820. I wrapped it around a tree in the spring of 1964, driving home from a party. I was just a little drunk and after I hit the tree I was still sitting there cranking the starter . . . I didn't even know I'd totaled the damn thing.

My license was suspended for thirty days and I was fined $25.10 for 'violation of the laws of the road.'

That same spring, Dave Talbot, a good friend and college bridge partner, said, 'Let's go on a rally.'

I asked him, 'What's a rally?'

So off we went to do The Rebel Yell Rally in an MGA we borrowed from a fraternity brother. The event was organized by Frank Churchill, an oil distributor in Middlebury, and the co-founder, with Dick Knudsen from Maine, of the MG 'T' Register which probably still exists today. It was a club for owners of old MGs. Frank was very instrumental in getting me interested in rallying. He gave me copies of old events to practice and was very supportive.

Talbot and I rallied together through 1965 and part of 1966 in a high performance Mustang, but we never did very well . . . always seemed to shoot ourselves in the foot somewhere along the way. I also won a few parking lot gymkhanas which were the forerunners of today's SCCA solo events.

I used to spend a lot of time driving down to Green Mountain College, about thirty miles south of my school, because the girls were very friendly and it was right on the border of New York where eighteen-year-old kids could drink. That was where I met Vicki Gauntlet. We were married between my junior and senior years.

Vicki was from Kalamazoo, Michigan, and that's where we got married. Her mother was an Upjohn and of course the family was very wealthy, but I was not sophisticated enough to understand all that back then. I just knew her as Vicki Gauntlet, not as Vicki 'Upjohn' Gauntlet, but the newspapers and magazines never failed to mention the Upjohn connection when they mentioned her.

We began rallying together after we were married.

I first discovered speed rallies in 1966 when Talbot and I took our Mustang to the Canadian Winter Rally in Toronto. I went to the Mobil dealer where I pumped gas (both Vicki and I had jobs back then) and got a set of Mobil spiked tires. Then I realized I'd need a front wheel driven odometer (to avoid falsely inflating the recorded mileage due to the spinning of the rear tires in the ice and snow) so I got a big steel hubcap and took it to an old Vermonter. He bolted a piece of oak to each side and drilled a hole through it. We used oak so it wouldn't overheat. We stuck an odometer cable through the hubcap and ran it up through a hole in the hood, then welded a little piece on the grease cap to drive a mechanical Halda mileage counter.

We had no idea what the hell we were doing. Eight hours after starting the two-day Canadian Winter Rally we exceeded the four-hour allowed lateness because we couldn't hold the required speeds, got lost a few times, and drove into a few snowbanks—we went home.

Rallying and partying seemed to occupy most of my time during my final year at Middlebury. After I graduated, Vicki and I lived in Stowe, Vermont, and she had enough money so I just became a worm—I didn't do a damn thing.

I intended to be a math teacher but Vietnam was on then and I owed some time to the army because I'd been in ROTC in college. So I entered the army as a lieutenant and they sent me to Germany.

I certainly never thought about rallying as a long-term commitment. It was just something fun to do on a Saturday night."

*4.3 1982 Hunsruck Rally (Germany): JB uses all the road—and a bit more, in his Talbot Sunbeam-Lotus. (Photo: Hugh W. Bishop)*

# 5
## Stuffum Buffum
### Don't Stand In The Ditches

**W**HEN JOHN BUFFUM returned to the U.S. from Germany with his wife and young daughter in the spring of 1969 he was about to learn the truth of Napoleon Bonaparte's warning, "Glory is fleeting, but obscurity is forever."

He was a twenty-five-year-old father when he was discharged as a first lieutenant and moved his family into a small house in Grand Isle, Vermont. In his words, "I hadn't done dick so far in life."

Few people in North America were even aware he had driven any rallies in Europe, much less finished twelfth overall on the famed Monte Carlo Rallye.

Soon after his return to civilian life he borrowed enough money to purchase a used car dealership in Burlington, Vermont, in partnership with Paul Choiniere, a friend he'd met at local rallies.

P-J's Auto Village opened in 1969 and soon acquired Triumph and Saab franchises. The partnership was quite successful with John handling parts and service and Paul managing sales. Later, as business increased, John also took over the accounting duties.

Triumph was soon replaced with little known Mazda, whose franchises were virtually free of charge.

In the fall of 1969, with the new business well on its way, JB began to look for other diversions.

It was Press On Regardless Rally time in Michigan . . . .

**JB:** "I decided to try the POR because I'd heard it was going to be a fast rally with a few closed stages. It was a great event in those days. It started and ended in Alma, Michigan, and had substantial sponsorship from Total Gasoline Company.

I first called Tom Grimshaw in Texas to co-drive (navigate) for me but he'd already committed to a ride so I called Harry Ward. I really didn't know either of them but I'd heard their names, especially in connection with the POR which both had already run for several years. Luckily, Ward wasn't doing anything and he agreed to go with me.

I loaded my Porsche into an eighteen-foot truck that I'd bought to go racing and took it to Michigan to practice. The day before the start we went up north near Camp Grayling and I high-centered the car in the deep sand on some tank testing road. We had to dig it out. It was not a good beginning.

I didn't know anybody in U.S. rallying back then. At one point during the rally I passed a yellow Mustang stuffed off the road in the rain.

Harry said, 'Oh good.'

I asked what he meant and he said, 'That was Gene Henderson we just passed.'

I said, 'Who the hell is Gene Henderson?' and he replied, 'He won this rally last year.'

Later we blew past Scott Harvey, then I stuffed us off the road and he passed us back.

There were four stages in the Lower Peninsula that year. They were timed to the nearest fifteen seconds. The rest of the rally was timed to the whole minute. We beat Harvey, and everyone else on all four stages, but only took a few points off

Scott. Then we lost fourteen minutes when I slowed down to miss a tree branch hanging over the road on a long sandy hill, and then couldn't make it to the top. He beat us by eight points."

The second place finish on the 1969 Press On Regardless Rally would be noted as John Buffum's first impact on high speed performance rallying in North America. But it could also have been the beginning of a string of escapades that would earn him his nickname some years later . . . "STUFFUM BUFFUM!"

The origin of the sobriquet "Stuffum Buffum" is unknown. Perhaps, because of John's early driving style, it occurred to several journalists and observers at the same time. It did have a certain heroic ring to it.

Certainly it must be said that Buffum's well-documented off road excursions during his early years fully justified the title.

Even in later years, when he was at the peak of his career, the 1981 official program for England's RAC World Championship Rally warned spectators about his driving style, "Good entertainment, but don't stand in the ditches."

When JB first appeared on the North American rally circuit he was banzai-quick and aggressive to a fault. There is an old adage in stage rallying: "If you crash, at least be leading, or it won't be worth it." JB often crashed—but he was usually leading.

Many a driver asked his co-driver, "Who the hell was that?" when JB careened past them in the middle of a stage, using all the road and a bit more and attacking every corner like it was a personal affront to his masculinity.

The wise co-driver would answer, "That is John Buffum. Do not chase him. Just wait."

A few miles further on the same driver might again ask,

*5.1 JB and Triumph: "Good entertainment, but don't stand in the ditches."*

"Who the hell was that?" as he caught a glimpse of a car stuffed so far into the trees it seemed unreachable from the road.

The co-driver would then have the satisfaction of answering, "That is John Buffum again. I told you—just wait."

JB made a lot of co-drivers look very wise in those early days.

A researcher can follow Buffum's progression from "Stuffum Buffum" to "King of The Road" by simply reviewing the cryptic comments John made on his personal records beginning in 1972:

"Over the bank . . . Stuck in mud—beaver pond . . . Off the road . . . Up on our side . . . Backed off the road . . . Accident! . . . Hit the bank . . . Crash! . . . Rolled! . . .Went off! . . . Blew engine . . . Crashed car and sold it . . .Totaled the car . . . Rolled before the start . . . Crashed Bruno's [Kreibich] car

56

... Into the swamp ... Crashed in dust ... Lost gears and rolled ... Lost brakes—went off bridge ... Hit ambulance head on ... BIG ROLL on bad pacenote! ... Rolled on first stage .. . BIG CRASH! ..."

And the classic ..."Rolled on press stage before start" (three different times).

Stuffum Buffum indeed! Many of the above notes appear more than once! He was certainly a "natural" right from the start. His 1969 drives in Europe attest to that fact. But, perhaps he was just a bit over exuberant in those early years.

**JB:** "In college I totaled the first car I ever owned. I guess

*5.2 1975: JB (L) with Bob Hourihan discussing Buffum's cornering technique while practicing the day before the start of the Olympus Rally (Washington). JB and Vicki drove the uprighted Ford Escort to victory the following day.*

that experience sort of carried over in my rally career.

When I started rallying in 1972 and 1973 I already had quite a bit of racing experience but I did not have rally experience and I did not have the maturity to know when 'fast' was 'fast enough.'

I went out and tried to win every stage by as much of a margin as I possibly could.

I believe a great competitor has the ability to compete at the level of his competition while still having the desire within himself to advance one more click—one step above the rest. And that was my problem in the mid-seventies. I thought you had to continue driving at the ultimate 110 percent until you had a ten- or fifteen-minute lead.

I remember in February 1967, heavyweight champion Cassius Clay changed his name to Muhammad Ali before he fought challenger Ernie Terrell for the title—and Terrell refused to use Ali's new name. So Ali gave Terrell a terrible beating and taunted him throughout the fight, yelling at him, 'What's my name? What's my name?' The press chastised him, claiming that 'Cruel Ali, with all his skills, carried Ernie Terrell for several rounds to inflict unnecessary punishment.'

I used to repeat that phrase to myself on stages. 'What's my name? What's my name?' I wasn't satisfied beating everyone, I wanted to crush them. I wanted them to remember my name.

Of course, back then nobody ever said to me, 'Hey, look John, five minutes is plenty. Just ease along for a bit now and win this thing.'

Then I went through a transition about 1975 when I began to learn to drive with my head, and by 1983, I usually won by only one or two minutes, unless something unusual happened.

Back in the seventies there wasn't anyone in the U.S. with years of stage rally experience. The SCCA PRO Rally series only started in 1973 and drivers and co-drivers were growing up together. Co-drivers also thought you had to win by as much as possible.

We were all young and eager in those days.

Today we have very good experienced co-drivers running with young drivers and they can guide and mold the young drivers, tamp down their enthusiasm when needed and push them when necessary. We didn't have that advantage back then.

If I had joined the sport after it had been around long enough to develop experienced co-drivers in this country there may never have been a Stuffum Buffum—but there also may not have been a national champion named John Buffum.**"**

*6.1 1973: Buffum (L) and Bert Everett pick up the silver at the Mid-Ohio Camel GT Race. Note that Bert smokes a **cigar** while holding the race sponsor's brand of **cigarettes**.*

# 6

## Sign of the Zodiac
### Libra International Racing

*J* OHN BUFFUM IS NOT A MAN who can easily accept the everyday routines most of us so eagerly embrace as soon as we acquire a decent job, a mortgage, and a color television set.

Although P-J's demanded much of his time and energy it did not fulfill his need for competitive challenge.

Perhaps it was the remembered excitement following his Monte Carlo performance that caused him to look to motor sports as his salvation from the mundane. Or maybe it was just a natural extension of his daily involvement in the automotive business.

Whatever the reason, he soon discovered there was no ongoing series of high speed rallies in North America, so he decided to go racing, while continuing to enter the interesting rally now and then.

At the end of 1970, after fiddling around with a Mini Cooper in local sports car races, he decided to campaign a Ford Escort the following season because "nobody was racing anything like it in the U.S." He sent his mechanic, Denny Turpin, to England where he spent three months building a new Escort at Broadspeed Engineering. The car was flown to the U.S. the day before the Lime Rock TransAm race in 1971 and JB promptly crashed it in the rain when the throttle stuck as he crested a hill.

He made his next serious attempt to break into the world of professional sports car racing later that same year, driving a Porsche 914-6 for Ralph Meaney. He teamed with his Monte Carlo partner, Yogi Behr, and Porsche racing guru, Erwin Kremer. They finished eighth overall, and second in their class at the 24 Hours of Daytona and a month later Pete Conrad, Apollo 12 astronaut and the third man to step on the surface of the moon, joined JB and Yogi as the third driver at the 12 Hours of Sebring. An engine mount broke and they failed to finish.

When JB finished eighth at Daytona, his team had beaten a host of race drivers well known to fans throughout the country: Peter Gregg, Hurley Haywood, Sam Posey, Peter Revson, Jo Siffert, Derek Bell, and Vic Elford—the same man who had befriended the young amateurs at Monte Carlo in 1969.

Later that same year, Buffum started his own team—Libra International Racing. He picked the title because both he and Yogi Behr were born under the seventh sign of the Zodiac. Libra was headquartered at P-J's in South Burlington, Vermont.

Before the start of the '72 racing season, Denny Turpin returned to England with several bushel baskets full of parts from the Lime Rock crash and a new, faster Escort was built for Libra Racing.

JB shared driving duties with John Fitzpatrick in the new Libra Escort and they ran the 24 Hours of Daytona and the 12 Hours of Sebring, winning their class each time.

Later in the '72 season, the new Escort was trashed when JB was creamed on the starting grid in Mexico. The salvable bits and pieces of the '71 and '72 Escorts were combined to create Libra's first rally car which JB entered in the 1972 POR Rally.

In 1973 Libra formed an alliance with Bobcor Performance of Buffalo, New York and Bert Everett joined the team as the second driver. They did not run well in their first two races at Daytona and Sebring but sorted the car out before the first TransAm race at Road Atlanta.

In '73 the TransAm Series ran under FIA rules similar to those used in the IMSA Camel GT Series and the Bobcor/Libra Escort was forced to race in a class that included cars with much more powerful engines.

Despite the handicap, the team won their class in each of their five TransAm starts, and John Buffum won the Under Two Liter TransAm Championship.

Flush with their success of the previous season, Libra joined forces with Carl Hurtig in 1974. They purchased two BMW 3-liter CSLs for $30,000 each and prepared to challenge the Porsches in the IMSA Camel GT Series.

It soon became evident that the BMWs could race with the '73 Porsches but not with the new '74 model. By mid-year Hurtig Team Libra was in debt and was not enjoying the successes they had expected. Following a race in Mexico, the BMWs were sold to Mexican race teams and Buffum abandoned his budding career as a race driver.

*Competition Press & Autoweek* reported an incident in July 1974, in which JB inadvertently caused the disqualification of Mario Andretti from the 6 Hours of Watkins Glen World Championship of Makes.

Partway through the race the oil light came on in JB's car and, considering the price of a new race engine, he parked it in the grass at the far end of the track and took a seat on the nearest guardrail.

A short time later Mario Andretti's Alfa Romeo 33TT12 coasted to a stop with electrical problems and Mario joined JB as a spectator. During an informal press interview after the race, JB said, "I asked Mario if he had called a taxi. He kind of

*6.2, 3 1973: JB and the Bobcor/Team Libra Escort race car he drove from the wrong side. (Photo: F.P. Foltz Photo, Ltd.)*

smiled and soon four mechanics came out and worked on his Alfa and he went back into the race."

Andretti drove the Alfa to fifth place, despite the time lost on repairs, but the rules of endurance racing clearly stated no one but the driver was allowed to work on a car unless it was in the pits. Buffum's innocent remarks caused such a flap that the race stewards took statements from everyone in sight and determined that the Alfa mechanics had indeed worked on the car while it was parked in the grass.

Andretti and Alfa were disqualified.

Thirteen years later, in 1987, Mario Andretti's son, Jeff, joined Buffum and Tom Grimshaw to win Brock Yates' ten-day One Lap of America in an Audi Quattro. It is indeed a very small world.

JB continued to dabble in rallying between 1970 and 1974—doing a couple of events here and there, but he was learning a hard lesson—a driver cannot enter two rallies a year and expect to improve his performance. He was moderately successful on race tracks, doing twelve corners one hundred times, but on the 1,000 corners of a stage rally, one or two would catch him out and he'd stuff the car off the road. He was always very quick; it took much more experience to be very good.

**JB:** "In 1970 I teamed up with a friend, Gene Hauman, from New York and ran his personal Renault R16 on the POR Rally. Gene brought the car to me in Vermont and I torched it . . . literally tore it apart putting in a cage, Plexiglas windows, the whole bit. After the rally he took it back to Long Island, parked it in a bad part of town, called his insurance agent and reported it stolen.

Of course, it was really me—making a proper rally car. I thought I was improving it—Gene thought it should be scrapped.

Gene Henderson was rallymaster that year and used a Fiat

*6.4 The Hurtig/Team Libra BMW CSL.*

*6.5 1974: JB leaving the Plaza Hotel (New York) for another day at the office.*

as course opening car. He and several other teams got stuck on a sand hill on a power line road and we passed them all. Later we came up on Jack Deno in an Audi and he wouldn't move over, or he moved slower than I thought he should, and I nailed him right in the ass. Smashed his car and ruined our steering. Ten miles later we quit.

Deno threatened to sue me later and I told him, 'Come on, it's a rally. Screw off.'

I missed the '71 POR because of my racing schedule but I went back in '72 with the Libra Escort we'd built out of the remains of the two race cars I'd already destroyed.

I took Bill Potvin as my navigator that year. It was the first year the POR was included in the FIA International Championship for Makes and Lancia sent Harry Kallstrom in a Fulvia to get some easy points. John Davenport came in from England to navigate for Kallstrom.

Everyone who was anyone in North American endurance rallying entered that year but Kallstrom was heavily favored since he was the only internationally-rated driver in the field and he was driving a factory car.

Gene Henderson entered two factory-sponsored Jeep Wagoneers. He drove one and Erhard Dahm, a German BMW dealer from Michigan, drove the other.

Dodge entered three Colts under the management of Tom Samida, a Kelsey-Hayes Michigan brake engineer who had previously won the POR.

The rally started on Belle Isle, near downtown Detroit. We won the first stage and had a 1.4-minute lead over Kallstrom by the middle of the first night in the Lower Peninsula of Michigan. Then on Hayes Tower Road I went into a tee right just a bit too quickly, got a little sideways, and *puff*—hit a stump and rolled.

Some spectators put us back on our wheels before we could get out of the car and I began to motor away when Potvin started yelling he'd lost the new watch his wife had just given him. So, back we go to the tee and look around for Potvin's watch, until I finally said, 'Screw this, we're leaving.'

Potvin lost his watch and the roll dropped us from first to nineteenth.

At another point I lost the road and ended up on the wrong side of a line of big trees. I had to drive through a field on the wrong side of the trees for half a mile before I could bust through and get back to the road. Still, we only lost thirteen seconds to Kallstrom on that stage. We worked our way back to seventh by the end of the first night.

During the second night, in the UP, there was a light snow on the ground and the Escort's throttle stuck wide open. We continued by turning the ignition key on and off and finally, **puff**—again—I stuffed us into a sand bank and sheered the splines off the steering wheel.

We threaded a nut onto the steering column and used a lug wrench to drive out of the stage, but with no steering wheel we had to call it a day. We'd been sitting fourth overall.

Kallstrom lost his brakes the second night and rolled the Lancia on the Germfask Truck Trail Stage. The car was totaled, but John Davenport salvaged a full bottle of scotch whiskey which they shared with Paul McClennan and Tom Grimshaw after they'd also crashed their Dodge Colt just down the road.

A Swede, a Brit, a Canadian and an American—sitting in the Michigan woods drinking a bottle of scotch . . . the Europeans certainly knew how to rally!

Gene Henderson won the rally in a four-wheel-drive Jeep Wagoneer. It marked the first ever win by a four-wheel-drive vehicle in international competition.

We didn't know it then but it was a hint of things to come—many years later. **"**

Buffum entered a total of nine rallies in the three year span from 1972 to 1974. He finished three, but he never won.

**JB:** "As a race driver I was never fantastic. In 1972, 1973 and 1974 I was a good driver but not quite good enough. I always believed there were other drivers faster than me.

Then I went rallying because I enjoyed it so much more. The challenge of the unknown makes rallying much more exciting than road racing.

*6.6 1972 POR (Michigan). JB and Bill Potvin on the opening Belle Isle stage, before the roll and other crashes that resulted in a lug wrench threaded onto the steering column in place of the steering wheel, and a DNF. (Photo: Peter Richardson)*

A road racer does about twelve turns one hundred times each. He tries to do those twelve corners exactly right each time—to duplicate his line.

Race drivers win through perfection of a very limited number of corners.

Rally drivers also strive for perfection but what they really hope to do is lose less time than everyone else.

A rally driver only sees each corner one time. You decide in advance what each will do and then, as you get into it, if it tightens—shit!—You scramble through it and lose time. Or you go into another corner thinking it is very tight and it opens up and—shit! again—you could have gone through it much faster.

In rallying you do twelve hundred corners one time, and that is what makes it so much more exciting . . . the unknown.

I like the feeling of being able to slide a car yet have total control over it. It looks like the car is totally out of control, but it's not. It's sliding and (in the case of a rearwheel drive car) I'm controlling it with my throttle foot.

When you do it just right it's a great feeling."

Although John and Vicki were divorced in 1974, they remained friends and continued to rally together for three more years (splitting expenses until they finally acquired some sponsorship).

John had quit racing by the end of '74 and was about to concentrate on professional stage rallying. He was on the threshold of the most remarkable rally career ever recorded in North America and was about to begin work on a world record for most victories in major championship rallies.

JB had made a down payment on his dues and would continue to pay them for years to come.

But he was about to begin collecting on his investment—with a vengeance!

# PART TWO

*The John and Vicki Show. Celebrating their 1976 victory on the Olympus (Washington) Rally. The Puyallup Daffodil Festival sponsored the NARA championship event—thus the flying flowers.*

# 7

## Let's Boogie
### The John and Vicki Show

*I*N 1975 PROFESSIONAL RALLYING took a significant step towards legitimacy in North America when David Ash, publisher and editor of SCCA's *Sports Car* magazine, turned his formidable marketing talents to the burgeoning PRO Rally Series and acquired national sponsorship from Lancia of America and Wonder Muffler Corporation.

Lancia had been absent from the U.S. market for eight years but had always been a strong contender in world championship rallying. In fact, they had won the World Championship for Manufacturers in 1974 and would repeat their victory in 1975.

Lancia decided to highlight their return to the showrooms of America by sponsoring the SCCA National PRO Rally Championship Series.

Wonder Muffler, a one-year-old, after-market exhaust company headquartered in East Orange, New Jersey, shared equally in the sponsorship as a promotional vehicle for their growing nationwide dealer organization. In addition to their cash support, they offered free exhaust systems to every PRO Rally competitor.

Professional rallying was also continuing to grow in Canada as Castrol Oil took on full sponsorship of the national championship series north of the border. It was an association that was to last for several years.

Stage rallying was about to burst onto the motor sports scene in North America and John Buffum, having made the decision to give up racing and concentrate on professional rallying, was more than ready for the challenge.

John and Vicki, decided to team up for the '75 season, again splitting expenses. They hired "Salty" Sottolano, the army buddy who had serviced for JB on the 1969 Monte Carlo Rallye, as their chief mechanic. Salty ran the Libra International Racing service crews for eleven successful years.

When John and Vicki began the '75 season, entering their 1971 Porsche 911 Carerra in the Perce Neige Canadian National Championship Rally, JB had yet to win his first major stage competition.

Their initial effort was less then memorable as JB stuffed the Porsche into a snowbank and DNFed.

In February John and Vicki returned to Canada to challenge North America's best on the two day, 734-mile (including 210 stage miles), twenty-third running of the British Empire Motor Club's Canadian International Winter Rally .

**JB:** "The '75 Canadian Winter Rally ran twenty-eight straight hours in temperatures ranging from minus 25° to minus 30°. We ran many of the stages more than once and they became polished skating rinks—very treacherous.

Toward the end of the rally we were running the long stages in the north where they now run the Tall Pines Rally— the Bancroft, Baptiste Lake area. We were sixty miles from the finish and John Paul Perusse, who had won the three previous Winter Rallies and would go on to become the 1975 Canadian National Champion, had us by about eight minutes in his Fiat 128 Abarth and then he stuffed it off, handing us a two-minute lead with two stages left.

To reduce weight Jean Paul threw everything out of his car that he could—spare tire, tools, jack, parts, everything— but

74

he couldn't catch us and we won the rally by 74 seconds. We had one bad moment on a corner I knew was coming up. Even though I expected it we did a 180-degree spin backwards into a snow bank. Luckily it was frozen solid and we bounced off, leaving tail pipes and rear bumper behind.

It was my very first major win and the beginning of the list of victories that brought me the world record twelve years later.**

**W**hat later became known as "The John and Vicki Show" began challenging for the U.S. National Championship with a win on Michigan's 20 Stages Rally. By virtue of his earlier victory on the Canadian Winter Rally, JB was listed as a Seed One Driver and started the rally first on the road, despite the fact he'd never entered a single U.S. PRO Rally. (It didn't take much to be a Seed One driver in the U.S. in those days.)

Two factors worked in the Libra team's favor in Michigan. First, the course was covered with deep snow and second, the organizers included a unique thirty-minute "free lateness" rule in the event regulations.

During the transit to the start of the first loop of ten stages, the Buffum/Vicki Porsche and Hourihan/Shepherd Volvo parked off route, as their closest rival, Jim Walker, driving a Volvo 142S, unknowingly passed by. After waiting for several other rally cars to pass, the "outlaws" returned to the course about sixteenth in line. Their strategy was to let the front runners knock down the heavy snow, allowing them a clear shot at the stage roads. As an added bonus, the front runners would not be able to check their stage times until the rally was half over. It was a calculated risk.

It was also a remarkable ploy, considering the fact that John and Vicki were relatively inexperienced compared to the rest of the field—and it worked. JB won seven of the opening

ten stages—averaging 65 mph on the snow-covered roads—
and hung on to take first overall by 39 hundredths of a minute
(23 seconds) over Walker's Volvo.

They followed up with a first overall in Washington's
Olympus Rally, using Libra's Ford Escort RS 1600.

The Olympus Rally was another page in the "Stuffum
Buffum" saga as JB put the Escort on its roof while practicing
the day before the start. Still, the following day, after some
quick overnight work by Salty and crew, he was able to post a
ten-minute victory over a very tough field.

By mid-season the national motor sports publications
were beginning to take note of professional rallying in North
America, and David Abrahamson, managing editor of *Car and
Driver* magazine, accepted an invitation to co-drive for JB on
the Marathon 400 PRO Rally in northern Michigan. His article
"Green Grows the Navigator" appeared in the December 1975
issue of *C & D:*

"First a confession: I now know that when I read in a
car at speed, I tend to vomit—a lot. And there's no way
you can serve as a navigator in a professional performance
rally without reading: mostly an odometer (calibrated in
hundredths of a mile) and a route book filled with cryptic
instructions that, in times of real trouble, have to be
deciphered and relayed to the driver every five or so
seconds. And this was not your everyday tweedy-jacket-
with-patches time/speed/distance kind of rally. Forget
about bug-eye Sprites in suburban Connecticut, stop-
watches and buck-toothed girl friends as co-pilots. Instead, try to picture a herd of race-prepared coupes and
sedans (280Zs, BMW 2002s, Datsun 510s, Dodge Colts),
equipped with killer engines and armored with enormous
skid pans, thrashing along wooded trails in an all-out race
for a low elapsed time. That's performance rallying. . . ."

After vomiting his way through most of the stages,

Abrahamson finally vacated the co-driver's seat and was replaced by one of JB's mechanics. Two stages from the end of the event, JB impaled the Escort on a stout tree stump and DNFed.

Bob Hourihan, a Michigan driver campaigning a Volvo 142S, won the rally (his only U.S. PRO Rally victory) after Hendrik Blok, a Dutch driver who had moved to California in 1964, ran out of gas two stages from the finish line—while leading! After the first five events of the 1975 season, Hourihan,and his young co-driver, Doug Shepherd, held the lead in the championship point standings. Past national champion, Scott Harvey, was second, and John Buffum was third.

But Buffum was on a roll and would not be stopped. He and Vicki, now Vicki Dykema—married to John Dykema, a Kalamazoo, Michigan banker—took their Escort to The Happiness Is Sunrise (HIS) PRO Rally in Olean, New York and stomped the competition, winning twelve of the thirteen stages on the dusty Allegheny Mountain roads.

On one stage, JB caught and passed the series point leader, Bob Hourihan, blew a tire, drove the final three miles on a flat—and still posted fastest time!

JB and Vicki moved into the lead in the national point standings.

They continued their drive towards the national title in Terlinqua, Texas—a ghost town located in the Big Bend country close to the U.S.- Mexico border. Until the PRO Rally Series arrived on the scene, Terlinqua was known only as "The Chili Cook-Off Capital of the World." Much of the surrounding desert lands were owned by racing legend, Carroll Shelby—a Texas chili fanatic of some renown.

The daytime temperatures on the rough, rocky stage roads reached 120° as JB drove the Libra Escort to a comfortable five-minute victory over Hendrik Blok's Datsun 510. Blok was later disqualified for short-cutting the course and violating road closure safety ribbons. The volatile Blok claimed total innocence but the colorful pennants wrapped around his Datsun at the following service area sealed his fate. He immediately quit PRO Rallying forever and mailed his competition license to the SCCA—an act that was to be repeated three more times during the coming years.

The rough Texas desert took its toll on the Libra Escort and JB switched to the '71 Porsche for the next event, Canada's most prestigious rally, The FIA International Criterium du Quebec. The Porsche's "Carerra" insignia had been replaced with the words "Let's Boogie."

JB finished the 1,000-mile-event with a fifteen-minute cushion over the second-place car. It was his most important victory to date, and one that finally proved the team was a major force in stage rallying as they soundly defeated the largest field ever assembled for an FIA International stage rally in North America, including two Canadian National Champions (Walter Boyce and Jean Paul Perusse) and England's Keith Billows in a works Ford Escort fitted with an 1800cc BDA engine.

One strange story highlighted the post party celebration at the Criterium: While sitting at the start line of a selective, JB and Vicki were passed by a pickup truck towing a Formula Vee race car. The racers were apparently lost but were allowed to drive onto the road.

The Libra Porsche was held an extra five minutes—but it wasn't enough. They caught the truck and trailer midway through the stage and were forced to stop and politely request the racers move aside and let them pass on the narrow road.

The affair cost the team a minute on the stage but John Buffum became the only rally driver to ever pass a formula race car on a stage in North America—a dubious achievement at best.

In addition to becoming the fastest, and certainly the most flamboyant rally driver in North America, Buffum was also learning the value of public relations. He arrived in Chillicothe, Ohio for the start of the Sunriser 400 PRO Rally sporting a complete new paint job on the Libra Escort—a red, white, and blue American flag scheme complete with white stars and American flags flying from each corner of the front windscreen. The car was aptly named "The Bicentennial Special." All this on a British car with the steering wheel on the wrong side.

The flagship Escort drew a lot of attention, as did Buffum's two-and-a-half-minute victory over Scott Harvey's new Dodge Colt. The largest starting field ever assembled for a U.S. PRO Rally (sixty cars), including the best in North America, had gathered in Ohio to stop "The John and Vicki Show" . . . and failed.

With four championship events remaining on the calendar, John Buffum and Vicki had already won the 1975 driver and co-driver national championships—during their first full year of competition.

Ohio was also the team's final U.S. victory in 1975.

In November JB and Vicki took their Bicentennial Escort to Michigan's Press On Regardless PRO Rally—the one event every North American rally driver wanted to win. JB was the odds on favorite but he was expecting a serious challenge from Polish National Champion, Sobieslaw Zasada, driving a factory prepared Porsche Carrera.

By the end of the third stage of the rally, all but one of the favorites were out of contention, leaving Zasada with a commanding lead.

Buffum rolled his car on Mt. Marquette and stayed in his belts as spectators put the Libra Escort back on its wheels. He later withdrew because of broken motor mounts. Scott Harvey, three time winner of the POR, parked his feather-weight four-wheel-drive Dodge Ramcharger with a seized engine. Gene Henderson, also a previous three time winner, sheared the distributor drive in his brand new Jeep CJ-7. BMW driver, Erhard Dahm, suffered a spectacular crash when, thinking a young spectator was about to step onto the road, he turned directly into the woods at 80 mph! Zasada loafed to an easy win.

While rally teams were battling each other on the very demanding POR roads of Michigan's Upper Peninsula a life and death struggle was taking place in Lake Superior, not far off the U.P. coastline. The *Edmund Fitzgerald*, a 729-foot oreboat, sank during a vicious storm, resulting in the deaths of twenty-nine crew members. It was called "the worst Great Lakes disaster in seventeen years."

*7.1 1975: JB and Vicki pose with "The Bicentennial Special" Ford Escort before starting the Sunriser 400 PRO Rally (Ohio). The flagship Escort finished first overall.*

The "Wreck of the Edmund Fitzgerald" was later immortalized in song by Canadian balladeer, Gordon Lightfoot—a cousin of Paul McClennan, who won the 1966 Shell 4000 Rally!

Buffum finished his first championship season with a win at Canada's Tall Pines Rally and a DNF in Green Bay, Wisconsin where he spun off in the snow on the El Diablo PRO Rally—the final event of the year. At the close of his first full year of professional rally competition, JB had won eight of the fourteen rallies he had entered.

It was obvious in 1975 that JB had adopted a new "image" as he appeared in several advertisements with collar length hair, bushy mustache, railroad engineer's cap, and red bandanna wrapped around his neck. Perhaps it could be said he went a bit too far when he appeared at one awards banquet wearing yellow leather pants!

As further proof that professional stage rallying was beginning to receive recognition as a major motor sport in the U.S., Kendall Motor Oils featured a full page ad on the back cover of the December 1975 issue of *Autoweek*. Its presentation of "The Winners Circle" included Al Holbert (IMSA), Don Garlits (NHRA and AHRA), Peter Gregg (IMSA Camel GT), Hurley Haywood (Camel GT Challenge), Bob Sharp (SCCA), and John Buffum (SCCA National PRO Rally Champion)!

It is also interesting to note that Nick Craw, current president of the Sports Car Club of America, Inc., appeared in the same ad, as the IMSA BFGoodrich Radial Challenge Series Champion.

Anyone laboring under the misapprehension that John Buffum's 1975 national championship was a one time fluke, was forced to reconsider when it was learned that Libra Racing had purchased Zasada's very fast works Porsche at the end of the POR rally.

JB and Miss Vicki would be back in 1976—but major disruptions and changes were about to take place in U.S. rallying.

*7.2 FIA International Criterium du Quebec Rally: JB and Vicki in the winning "Let's Boogie" Porsche Carerra. (Photo: Matt Jerue)*

# 8

# The Sanctioning War

## Only Show In Town

*I*N THE DECEMBER, 1975 ISSUE OF *Road & Track* magazine, Cameron Warren wrote, in his article titled "PRO Rally Series Wrap-up":

"As sanctioning body, and somewhat reluctant overseer of the sport, the SCCA has been the target of a certain amount of flak. Still, they are the logical organization for the job, and it is unlikely a rival group could engender enough additional strength to make it worthwhile."

Warren's timing was unfortunate since his article appeared at the same time the motoring press announced the formation of a rival sanctioning body, the North American Rally Association (NARA).

While NARA did not formally appear until December 1975, the planning actually began at the conclusion of an earlier meeting in Olean, New York on August 10th, following the awards banquet for the SCCA's Happiness Is Sunrise PRO Rally.

When the SCCA first announced national sponsorship for its 1975 National PRO Rally Series, the news was met with great enthusiasm by event organizers and competitors. Professional stage rallying was finally coming of age in America.

However, by mid-year the enthusiasm had given way to

growing resentment of SCCA's lack of material support for the sport. Many people believed the SCCA had simply pocketed the sponsors' money and done little else. They could see very little, if any, benefit to rallyists.

The August meeting between SCCA officials and PRO Rally participants was supposed to settle differences between the two groups. It didn't.

One other factor was to decide the outcome of the Olean meeting. David Ash, for many years the publisher of SCCA's membership magazine, *Sports Car*, had just been informed that his contract would not be renewed in 1976. Ash was not pleased and Ash held the keys to the sponsors of SCCA's National PRO Rally Series.

Organizers and competitors left the Olean meeting with a single message from the SCCA, "We are the only sanctioning body for professional rallying in the United States. If you don't like what we're doing that's too damn bad. We're the only show in town." While these words were not actually verbalized by SCCA officials, it was a fair summation of their attitude. It was a mistake.

Before the end of the 1975 season, David Ash formed a rival sanctioning body (NARA) with a Board of Stewards consisting of John Buffum, Gene Henderson, Bob Hourihan, Tom Grimshaw, John Nagel, Ron Richardson, and Ian Tugwell. In addition, Ash also spirited away SCCA's sponsors, Lancia and Wonder Muffler, and added Pirelli Tires for the NARA series. To add insult to injury, Ash signed most of the important U.S. stage rallies for his new series in 1976.

And he sued SCCA for breach of contract over his loss of *Sports Car* magazine. In other words, David Ash declared war on the SCCA.

In February, NARA held its first national convention at the Hyatt Regency in Dearborn, Michigan, to kick off its inaugural season, dubbed the "America's Cup Championship Series." It was a significant meeting because it was the first time many organizers from opposite ends of the country had ever met each other, and it began the much needed process of standardization of professional rallying in America.

SCCA retaliated for Ash's lawsuit by obtaining a federal court injunction to stop NARA's sanctioning activities and, in particular, its opening event in April—The Pirelli Olympus Rally in Olympia, Washington. The SCCA was understandably upset since the Olympus, sponsored by the Puget Sound Sports Car Club, had previously been an SCCA National Championship event.

Ash struck back with an offsetting court order which allowed the Olympus to take place as scheduled.

In May, SCCA and NARA met in the U.S. District Court in New Haven, Connecticut. Cameron Argetsinger, executive director of the SCCA, opened the hearing with a full day of testimony which did little to enhance SCCA's position since it soon became apparent Argetsinger had very limited knowledge of the sport and its relationship to his own organization.

NARA attorneys eagerly awaited cross-examination of Argetsinger but SCCA attorneys announced at the end of the first day that, "for reasons too confidential to discuss in open court," their client could not return for cross-examination for at least two weeks.

The presiding judge was livid and delivered a scathing damnation of SCCA's delaying tactics.

Within a week SCCA and NARA reached an out-of-court agreement dropping all lawsuits. SCCA agreed to stop harassing NARA. NARA agreed not to use the words "PRO Rally" which SCCA claimed as their own registered trademark. From then on NARA referred to all its events as "performance rallies" or "rally races."

Meanwhile, contingency sponsors were upping the ante for professional rallies in both national series and "The John and Vicki Show" was still rolling over the competition . . . .

**JB:** "I think I came in at just about the right time, in the middle of the seventies. In 1973, when the SCCA national championship series began, rallying was a very small and unknown sport in the U.S. It was just beginning and wasn't much of anything—still very much a 'privateer sport.'

Then in 1976 David Ash stepped in and started a new sanctioning body in competition with the SCCA. It was a very good thing for professional rallying in our country. The sport continued to grow substantially into the eighties primarily because the competition between the two sanctioning bodies gave it a jump-start.

At the start of my second full season (1976) I decided to concentrate my efforts on NARA's America's Cup National Championship Series because I thought David Ash was taking a much more professional approach to the sport than SCCA and because NARA had acquired most of the top U.S. events and all the major sponsorship.

Also in 1976, the SCCA and Canada's sanctioning body, the Canadian Automobile Sport Clubs (CASC), announced a combined North American Rally Cup Championship. So, to qualify for the new championship, I ran two SCCA events in 1976—The Allegro and The El Diablo—and won both of them to go along with two wins and a second in Canada to take the first combined North American Rally Cup Championship."

JB entered fourteen U.S. and Canadian professional rallies during his second full year of competition. He won eight of them; two in Canada, four in the NARA series, and two in the SCCA series.

For the second year in a row he was America's national champion—but this year it was a NARA championship rather than an SCCA championship. Hendrik Blok, "The Flying Dutchman" from California, won the SCCA championship—despite the fact he had quit professional rallying "forever" after his disqualification the previous year in Texas.

86

In reviewing NARA's first year as a national sanctioning body, it certainly appeared it had emerged as the dominant regulating force in U.S. professional rallying. The SCCA's National PRO Rally Championship Series was reduced from twelve events in 1975 to six in 1976—compared to NARA's nine events the same year. SCCA attracted a total entry of 188 teams in 1976, while NARA events started a total of 395 teams.

Probably the most telling fact was that the SCCA sponsored its own professional rally series while NARA enjoyed national sponsorship from Lancia, Pirelli and Wonder Muffler.

During the 1976 season John and Vicki used the ex-works Porsche purchased from the Polish national champion at the end of the '75 POR as their primary ride, but they also resurrected the old Escort to take a win in Canada on the Piston Les Wapitis Rally in Quebec and JB drove a Toyota to a second place finish on the Highlands Rally in Nova Scotia.

**JB:** "Walter Boyce was driving for Toyota Canada in 1976 and was complaining about the Celica so Robin Tyler, the crew chief for Toyota, asked me to drive it on the Highlands Rally. They put Canadian, Doug Woods, with me as co-driver.

We had a really tight battle with Jean Paul Perusse's Fiat and near the end his co-driver, John Bellefleur, lied to us about their score—dropping a full minute from their total stage times. Halfway through the final stage we had a flat and I thought, *This car hasn't finished a rally in a year. Better second than another DNF.* So I slowed way down and finished second behind Perusse.

Actually, considering the lost minute, we could have won, even with the flat tire, if I had continued at a reasonable pace."

The SCCA/NARA war came to a head in Michigan when NARA scheduled its new Marquette 1000 Rally on the same

November weekend as SCCA's Press On Regardless. Both events were located in Michigan's Upper Peninsula. It was a sign of the times when the SCCA was forced to cancel the POR, its most important annual event, because nearly every top competitor in the U.S. opted for NARA's Marquette 1000!

The NARA event, organized by Doug Shepherd, turned into a bit of a fiasco when forty teams exceeded time-bar and were eliminated the first night by a competitor who became stuck in the deep sands of the U.P. and blocked the course. Only eight teams were allowed to start the final night. Buffum DNFed when he slid straight off the road four miles into the Spaulding Tower Stage and veteran driver, Gene Henderson won the rally in a factory backed Jeep CJ-7.

Today, the 1976 cancellation marks the only year in its forty-four year history that the POR did not officially take place. However, in honor of its past glories, Bob Hourihan organized an "unofficial" POR the night prior to the start of the Marquette 1000. At midnight, ten drivers each threw five dollars into an empty beer glass (an appropriate receptacle for the prize fund of this hallowed event), enlisted wives, girlfriends and innocent bystanders as co-drivers, and dashed into the woods to drive their rally cars two times through a single snow-covered stage road.

As the instigator of the shortest POR in history it was only just that Hourihan emerged the winner.

JB and Vicki decided to cap their victorious year by entering England's RAC World Championship Rally . . . .

**JB:** "We picked up a little sponsorship from Pirelli, Zetachron and Filtron and decided to do the '76 RAC in a Ford Escort RS1600 we bought in England for about $7,000, and sold after the rally. Jean Paul Perusse also entered the RAC that year, driving a Saab with his Canadian co-driver, John Bellefleur, on board.

Our Escort wasn't very good. Pieces kept falling off it as

88

we went along. The rally was four days—1,800 miles, and more than 250 of the best rally teams in the world were entered. I just wanted to get into the top twenty finishing positions on my first RAC.

The man to beat that year was Sandro Munari, a factory driver in a Lancia Stratos. He'd already won at Monte Carlo, Portugal and Corsica, placed second in San Remo behind his teammate, Bjorn Waldegard, and third in Morocco. That year Lancia won the World Manufacturer's Championship for the third year in a row.

I had some decent stage times despite the car. On one stage I ran the fifth fastest time—one second behind Munari's Stratos.

During the Forest of Dean stages, early in the event, a German Porsche lost its brakes, went straight at a Tee junction and flew straight into the spectators. So they canceled the remaining Dean Forest stages and no one knew quite what to do. Will Sparrow was there in an experimental Vauxhall and once again Vicki's blonde hair helped us. He said we should follow him and he'd show us what to do. We followed him around with a group of other cars that ran an hour and a half behind the front runners who had gotten through before the accident. For twenty hours we just plugged along and booked in and booked right out of every rest stop.

Perusse and Bellefleur, running behind us, picked up sixty minutes road penalty when they checked into a control too early and were disqualified.

Then, after 1,600 miles and sixty-eight stages, the clutch broke while we were sitting in twentieth place overall—eight stages from the end of the rally.

England's Roger Clark won.

It was a great experience. In Birmingham we ran through Sutton Park, which is huge, like our Central Park in New York. It was estimated that 30,000 spectators were in the park and that two million people watched the entire rally.

At one point on the second half of the course we came over a hill and could see the Atlantic Ocean and about fifty miles of the English coastline. There was a big horseshoe-shaped bay and we were up high enough that we could see the whole thing. That was great.

Although we didn't finish, it was good experience for the coming years.**"**

At the close of 1976 John Buffum, two-time national champion and winner of the first combined U.S./Canadian North American Rally Cup, had established himself firmly as the man to beat in North America.

Despite the sixteen championship rally wins in two years, two national titles, one U.S./Canadian championship, the ever increasing national media exposure and a movie titled, *Rally Racing Fever* which featured their 1976 winning season, JB and Vicki were still buying their own rally cars and still paying their own expenses.

That was about to change.

# NORTH AMERICAN RALLY ASSOCIATION, INC.

## ANNOUNCES

*A Twelve Event Performance Rally Championship for the*

*with a minimum guaranteed cash purse of $2,500.00 per event*

### NARA'S 1976 Championship Competitions Schedule

| Date | Event | Start/Finish | Event Chairman | Organizer |
|---|---|---|---|---|
| April 16-17-18 | Pirelli Olympus | Olympia, Wash. | Tony Stelmack | Puget Sound Sports Car Club |
| May 1-2 | Lancia 20 Stages | Grayling, Michigan | Lee Rizor | Sports Car Club of Ann Arbor |
| May 15-16 | Wonder Muffler Northern Lights | Midland, Michigan | Jim Miller | Valley Rally Association |
| June 5-6 | Lancia Rim of the World | San Bernadino, Calif. | Ray Hocker | Ridgecrest Rally Club |
| • July 10-11 | Lancia Vegas 500 | Las Vegas, Nevada | | to be announced |
| August 13-14-15 | Pirelli Happiness Is Sunrise | Olean, New York | Al Burgasser | Western N.Y. Pro Rally Committee |
| August 28-29 | Wonder Muffler Bicentennial | Waco, Texas | Tom Grimshaw | Texas Sports Car Club |
| September 25-26 | Wonder Muffler Rip Van Winkle | Ellenville, New York | John Buffum | Catskill Pro Rally Club |
| October 9-10 | Pirelli Sisu 300 | Houghton, Michigan | Eric Lind | Michigan Rally Club |
| October 23-24 | Pirelli Trinity Alps | Sacramento, California | Ron Richardson | No. Cal. Performance Rally Assoc. |
| November 5-6-7 | Wonder Muffler Marquette 1000 | Marquette, Michigan | Doug Shepherd | Sports Car Club of Marquette |
| November 13-14 | Pirelli Mountaineer | Augusta, Maine | Steve Dorr | Sports Car Club of Maine |
| • December 4-5-6 | Lancia Mexican 1000 | Ensenada, Mexico | | to be announced |

* Tentative

If performance rallying is your bag - or you're a B Sedan driver with no place to go, NARA'S AMERICA'S CUP Championship has got to be what you're looking for. For more information, contact NARA'S National Office, P.O. Box 814, Nyack, N.Y. 10960 (914) 358-2599. For a copy of NARA'S official rules, send $2.50 to cover rules, handling and postage and get a free copy of NARA'S Rally Newsletter.

---
**NORTH AMERICAN RALLY ASSOCIATION, INC.**
P.O. Box 814, Nyack, N.Y. 10960
Please send me:
☐ Full Details - No Charge
☐ Official Rules - I Enclose $2.50

Name _____

Address _____

City _____

State _____ Zip _____

---

*8.1 Opening salvo in the sanctioning war: NARA's national advertisement of the "America's Cup" Performance Rally Championship. Thirteen events were listed. Nine actually happened. Four were ficticious.*

*9.1 This photo of rally driver, John Buffum, and race driver, Bob Tullius, together with the rally, race, and street versions of the Triumph TR-8 was used in a national advertising campaign.*

# 9
# The Shape of Things to Come
## Years of Triumph

*Autoweek* magazine . . April 10, 1976:
"The factory-backed European rally version of the TR7 was introduced in England last week, just before the car goes on sale there, and moved experienced journalists to roll their eyes back in their heads and say 'ooooh!' A sample comment: 'Fantastic . . . handling as good as the Stratos and a lot easier to drive . . . startling times through the stages.'"

**B** Y THE END OF NARA'S FIRST complete year as a national sanctioning body, the edges were already beginning to unravel in the uneasy alliance between David Ash and his advocates. The loss of Wonder Muffler, which ran out of sponsorship funds halfway through the 1976 season; the cost of defending the SCCA lawsuit; and Ash's failure to sign new, often promised sponsorship deals, all contributed to a serious cash shortage in the new organization that could not match SCCA's more than 25,000 members.

Some event organizers received dunning letters demanding payment to NARA's insurance carrier—a cost that was to be covered entirely by the national office. The organizers were not amused.

Ash also created growing resentment among competitors when he introduced his self-styled "star system." His public relations ploy required involvement of a star on whom to focus media attention, and John Buffum, the only two-time national champion, and Miss Vicki, his pretty blond co-driver, who was, incidentally, an heiress to the Upjohn fortune, were the perfect choices. The older, more experienced competitors were not thrilled with the amount of attention lavished upon the relative newcomers.

Perhaps most disturbing of all was the fact that NARA was "owned" entirely by one man—David Ash, and he never revealed any hard financial facts to his troops, although he often bemoaned the thousands of "personal" dollars he was spending to keep NARA alive.

Still, because of his incredible vitality, cheerful optimism, and promotional genius, David Ash retained support from Lancia and Pirelli, added Porsche-Audi as a sponsor of selected rallies and announced a full twelve event schedule for 1977.

He also solved his financial problems by closing down "NARA" and opening a new organization titled "NARRA"— North American Rally Racing Association. NARRA actually staged only five events in 1977, compared to the SCCA's eight National PRO Rallys, but the little promotional genius from New York pulled off yet another major coup—he brought British Leyland into North American rallying and created a lot of renewed media interest in the sport over the next three years.

John and Vicki began the season in the same tired Porsche Carrera they had used to win the 1976 NARA and North American Rally Cup Championships. They took a first overall in SCCA's opening event, The Borax Bill Memorial, staged on rocky desert terrain bulldozed into "streets" to create a modern metropolis in Southern California. Instead it ended up as a sparsely-populated subdivision of six-thousand residents, called California City.

JB won eighteen of the twenty-one stages on The Borax Bill. His strongest competition, 1976 SCCA National Champion, Hendrik Blok, was forced to accept second place.

In the second SCCA event, The 100 Acre Woods Rally in Missouri (called by some, "the roughest rally ever run"), the Libra team again took overall honors while Blok broke his Dodge Colt and hard-charging newcomer, Danny Goodwin, an Alaskan state trooper, balanced his Alaskan Oil Company sponsored Mazda pickup truck, (quickly dubbed "The Moose Piss Special" by rally humorists) in the top of a thirty-foot tree.

Buffum's final drive in the old Porsche resulted in a win at the Puerto Rico 24 Hour Rally with Gene Hauman on board.Then finally—after two and a quarter years of running on their own dollar, John and Vicki signed a contract with British Leyland to campaign the new 4-cylinder, 16-valve, 1988cc, TR-7 in both the U.S. and Canadian professional rally series.

It was John Buffum's first professional rally contract and it was arranged by David Ash . . . .

**JB:** "I, and several other drivers, had agent agreements with David Ash in 1977 and he made the deal with Mike Cook of British Leyland to field a factory-backed team of two TR-7s in North America. I was to run the U.S. operation and Walter Boyce, five-time Canadian National Champion and the only North American driver to ever win a world championship rally (1973 POR), was to run the Canadian effort.

Triumph was just beginning their rally program in Europe and British Leyland built our cars in England and shipped them to us. Norm Busby, who had helped with the 1974 BMW racing program and worked for me on the '76 RAC Rally, came over from Leamington Spa, England to be our crew chief and Salty was still our chief mechanic. I got $50,000, plus parts, for our first year with Triumph, but I had to pay David Ash $15,000 for the dea—$10,000 as his fee, plus $5,000 as his percentage of the value of the parts.

In January I drove a stock TR-7 on the 18th Annual Tri-State 24-Hour Rally, with Rich Schneider as my navigator. It was a very fast TSD rally that ran 670 miles over ice and snow covered back roads in Maine, Vermont and New Hampshire. We finished first overall with a total penalty of one minute, three seconds. It was a tough rally and a good win for Triumph in the U.S. Much better than our first showing in stage rallying.

We introduced the new TR-7 in April at NARRA's Olympus Rally near Tacoma, Washington. British Leyland backed us with a lot of press and media hoopla—and we DNFed.

We started the first little spectator stage, went up D2900 Road, turned left at a crossroad and came back down about a mile. Hendrik Blok rolled his Dodge Colt at the crossroad, ran over to a spectator's new Colt, ripped the distributor cap out of it, put it into his rally car, and motored away.

Then we started a forty-five mile stage on Mima Creek in the Capital Forest and the ignition was getting wet from the numerous water holes we drove through. It was only the second stage and we already had about an eight-minute lead, but the Triumph was sputtering badly at the finish of the stage.

On the next transit, north of Brooklyn, I was trying to make up time, got 'caught out' at a ninety degree corner, slid into a ditch and bent a control arm and fender and couldn't continue. That corner was renamed 'The Shape of Things To Come'—Triumph's national advertising slogan.**"**

It wasn't a good beginning, especially since Mike Cook of British-Leyland was spectating.

It was also not a good beginning for the 1977 NARRA series as the cash payout on the Olympus fell far short of the announced prize fund.

## The Shape of Things to Come

The NARRA Rim of the World Rally in Palmdale, California was the site of JB's next misadventure with the new car . . . .

**JB:** "British Leyland decided to do a movie on North American rallying and our new team. It was titled "Buffum & Company." They did a lot of helicopter footage at The Rim where we were going along good, leading Blok's Colt. At one point in the movie I told Vicki to look out her window at the great scenery—a long way below us. She took one look over the edge and said, 'Oh shit!' It was cut out of the sound track but if you listen close you can almost hear her say it.

I lost second gear in the Triumph but kept limping along, staying close to Blok's times until I finally put us on our side on a tight turn that I tried to do in third gear, in the snow. We didn't have the strength to flop the car back onto its wheels and we DNFed once again, and Blok went on to win the rally."

In Pennsylvania JB spun the Triumph backwards into a ditch for his third DNF in a row at the SCCA's Susquehannock Trail PRO Rally. His old adversary, Jean Paul Perusse, ran his new factory backed 2-liter, 16-valve Saab 99 EMS, but a series of flat tires put him out of contention. Ohio driver, Erik Jones, won the rally in a Datsun 510.

The following week JB and Vicki experienced their fourth non-finish at NARRA's 20 Stages Rally in Michigan . . . .

**JB:** "Things went well for a while and we had a pretty good lead. Then, about halfway through the Mack Lake Tower Stage we broke the rear axle and limped into service. When the crew replaced the axle the brackets didn't quite match, but they jury-rigged it and we continued. Finally we hit a large bump and the axle came up and bashed the fuel pump, forcing us to park the car.

97

After we were out of the rally we hid in the weeds near the finish of a stage with a mechanic's creeper board. When Blok came flying by we held up the board, with its penned-in special message, and he shut down, thinking it was the finish line. His co-driver had to scream at Hendrik to get him going again. He still won the stage, but later blew an engine and also DNFed. I don't think Hendrik was amused by our trick. He was just too intense—didn't have a sense of humor when it came to rallying. **"**

**B**y mid-year it seemed the "sorting out" problems experienced by both the U.S. and Canadian Triumphs might continue to plague Buffum and Boyce and remove them from serious contention for any championship—SCCA, NARRA, CASC, or the North American Rally Cup. John Davenport, *chief supremo* of all British Leyland competition, traveled from England to see how his two cars were doing in North America.

The future did not look promising for the new Triumph rally program. But in June it all came together at the Piston les Wapitis in Quebec.

The factory-sponsored Toyota and Saab teams were mounting serious challenges in Canada. Taisto Heinonen was leading the CASC championship in his Toyota and Jean Paul Perusse was staying very close in his Saab.

The rally did not start out well for the Triumph team; Walter Boyce's car was badly damaged when a local resident ran a stop sign and T-boned it during a transit. Boyce suffered a broken collar bone that would require several weeks to heal.

But Buffum's TR-7 finally finished—fifty-four seconds in front of Heinonen and six minutes over third place Perusse. It was JB's first long awaited victory in the new TR-7 and the team celebration included a giant cake topped with a replica of the winning car.

JB's car was immediately shipped to California for the next SCCA event—the La Jornada Trabajosa in Bakersfield—where he posted his first U.S. victory for Triumph, beating Hendrik Blok's Dodge Colt by two and a half minutes on the very dusty roads of the Sequoia National Forest.

Things were certainly improving for Team Libra as JB drove the TR-7 to victory in the next four Canadian championship events in a row. On back to back weekends in July, he won the Highlands Rally in Nova Scotia and the Lobster Rally in New Brunswick, then followed up the next month with wins on the Mountain Trials and Rocky Mountain rallies in British Columbia.

The four consecutive victories locked up JB's second consecutive North American Rally Cup Championship, moved British Leyland-Triumph into first place in the Canadian Manufacturer's Championship, and left Buffum only four points behind Toyota's Taisto Heinonen for the driver's championship of Canada.

While JB and Vicki were running wild in Canada, the two U.S. series were getting very tight as fifty-eight teams—the second largest starting field of the year—fought it out on NARRA's Happiness Is Sunrise Rally in New York. Scott Harvey and Hendrik Blok joined in a fierce battle until Blok's Dodge Colt ran out of brake fluid, dropping him to thirteenth, giving Harvey his only win of the year.

In early September all three North American championship series took a breather as the international rally world turned its attention to the Criterium du Quebec—an FIA World Championship rally . . . .

**JB:** "In 1977 Fiat and Ford were locked in a good battle for the world championship and both factories wanted to win in Canada. There were five Fiat 131 Abarths and two 1800 RS

99

Ford Escorts entered on the Criterium. The rally started in Montreal on Thursday and finished back there on Sunday.

The Fiats were quickest on all the tarmac stages, including the laps around the Mont Tremblant Race Circuit, but the Fords seemed to be a bit better on the slippery forest stages.

Walter Rohrl was the fastest of the Fiat drivers but both he and Markku Alen lost their engines when the oil pump filter brackets broke and dumped all the oil out of their Fiats. Then Timo Makinen blew his Fiat's engine on the Mont Tremblant Circuit.

Ari Vatanen's Escort was leading going into the final night but he dropped out with a failed ignition system. At the finish Timo Salonen and Simo Lampinen were one-two in Fiats and moved Fiat within two points of Ford in the world championships. Roger Clark and Jim Porter finished third overall in a works Ford Escort.

Fiat eventually won the world championship that year.

The Criterium was 1,000-miles long with 450 stage miles. Some stages were over seventy-miles long on logging roads in the Laurentian Mountains. At one point we clubbed a big rock on a seventy-one mile stage and broke Vicki's seat mounts. By the end of the stage she had one broken and three severely cracked ribs. We got a medic to tape her up at a rest halt and motored on.

When we came out of Mont Tremblant Park it was just getting dark and our alternator had failed so we had no lights.I turned everything off and waited for Roger Clark in the next car and tried to follow him to the next service. But he wouldn't have any of that and pulled over and stopped, so we forged ahead as best we could to reach our service which was only a mile from the start of a seventy-mile foggy lake stage.

After service we arrived at the start control two minutes late. Shinizuka had been running behind us in a Colt and he was already into the control, but I gambled, ran in and asked for my correct minute—that had already gone by—and they gave it to me! I checked in after Shinizuka but received an in-time before him and they never caught on. I caught and passed him in the fog, about fifteen miles in, then the hood flew off the Triumph and I had to drive the rest of the stage with my right hand while I held the hood on the roof with my left and Vicki changed gears for me.

We finished fourth overall, first North American behind the European factory drivers. Walter Boyce finished right behind us in the other TR-7.**"**

At the Criterium awards banquet John Buffum thanked the European drivers for coming to Canada and closed by saying, "You set a standard of competitiveness for us in North America. If we could compete against rallyists of your caliber on a regular basis we would be a lot more proficient."

The U.S. rally battles resumed in late September and because of Vicki's Criterium injuries it was a good opportunity for Buffum to try a different co-driver . . . .

**JB: "**I wanted Vicki to finish out the '77 season but I also wanted to look for a new co-driver for the next year. Things were getting a bit trying between Vicki and me, but she had helped pay for the Escort and Porsche years in 1975 and '76 and I felt I owed her some payback, even though, at that point, I really didn't want a female co-driver sitting next to me.

I first considered Tom Grimshaw but he'd recently had a heart operation and we all thought he would not return to rallying. Then I considered Doug Woods, a very good Canadian co-driver who had done the Highlands Rally with me in '75. But Woods put too much emphasis on 'What are you going to pay me? We're big time professionals, etc., etc.'

101

*9.2 JB and Vicki and the first Triumph TR-7, on a stage of the 1977 Criterium du Quebec World Championship Rally. (Photo: Hugh W. Bishop)*

*9.3 JB holds the Triumph's hood, Vicki shifts the gears as the team finishes a stage and places fourth overall on the '77 Criterium.*

102

The other possibilities were Canadians Tom Burgess and Robin Edwardes, but Burgess was already running for Toyota with Heinonen, and Robin (who had co-driven with me back in '71, '72 and '73) and I could not seem to win together for some unknown reason. It was many years later before we finally won a rally together.

I finally settled on Doug Shepherd from Michigan. Doug had been running with Bob Hourihan. He was not very experienced but I felt I could live with that—teach him my system. He was intelligent, young, and enthusiastic—the gung-ho type who would work hard.

It turned out to be an excellent choice. We won a lot of rallies and several national championships during our years together.

My first rally with Shepherd was SCCA's Sunrise 400 in Ohio. We had a good run for a while. Harvey, Jim Walker, Hendrik Blok and I all traded stage wins, but I was having to pump the hell out of the brakes to make them work. We followed Blok out of a rest halt that didn't include service and it was pretty dusty. I was going a bit too fast for the conditions and there was a flat right that tightened hard into a bridge—we went straight off and DNFed.

Blok won the rally—for a while. The organizers had put in a sneaky speed observation control which caught most of the rally because it was on a wide paved transit road in a national forest and was an automatic 25 mph zone.

After all the confusion cleared away, Blok dropped to seventh and Ralph Brooks, a relatively unknown driver from Ohio, took the win in a Datsun 280Z, even though he hadn't won a single stage.

As usual, Mr. Blok went into orbit. He stayed in Chillicothe, Ohio for several days after the rally, threatening to sue everyone from the event chairman to the man who held the radar

gun. He even threatened to notify the authorities about use of
a radar gun by an unlicensed operator—which could have
caused serious problems for the sport. Finally he again quit
professional rallying 'forever,' mailed his competition license
back to the SCCA and flew home to California.**"**

**T**wo weeks later, Blok changed his mind again and won
the SCCA's Nor'wester PRO Rally in Issaquah, Washington.

By the end of October the Canadian national championship and both U.S. national championships were still up for
grabs. Only the combined U.S./Canada North American Rally
Cup Championship had been decided—in favor of John Buffum.

Everyone took a month off to prepare for the biggest
North American national rally of the year—the SCCA's Press
On Regardless in Michigan's Upper Peninsula. Every top
seeded rally driver in the U.S. and Canada showed up for the
'77 POR which hosted sixty-three teams—the largest starting
field of the year.

Taisto Heinonen grabbed an early lead with a win on the
seven and a half-mile opening stage but JB won the next three
and moved into first place.

On the fifth stage Buffum put his TR-7 into the trees and
lost eight minutes, giving the lead back to Heinonen. But
pressures were starting to tell on all the top teams as Heinonen
broke a rocker arm, Perusse's Saab went out with ignition
problems, Henderson flopped his Jeep CJ-7 onto its side,
Harvey broke the rear suspension, and Jim Walker ditched his
Volvo while leading late in the rally.

At one point Buffum decided to retire to the bar since he
was so far behind but his mechanic, Salty Sottolano, threatened him with bodily harm if he didn't push on.

Hendrik Blok, the "Flying Dutchman," was pushing his Dodge Colt beyond reasonable limits—averaging better than 78 mph on the Winslow Lake Stage—but Buffum was winning most of the stages, averaging 4 mph faster than Blok!

Blok finally won the rally but most of the excitement was centered on John Buffum's spectacular drive as he and Vicki finished third overall after restarting in twenty-third position following their off-road excursion and the tense conversation with his chief mechanic.

The upset victory in Michigan would have won the SCCA National PRO Rally Championship for Hendrik Blok except for a strategic mistake on his part. The SCCA rules allowed a driver to count his best five finishes out of his first seven starts during 1977, but it also allowed a driver to "non-declare" one event by notifying SCCA, prior to the start, that the driver did not want to count the rally as one of his seven starts.

Blok, realizing that every heavy hitter in North America, including most of the past POR winners, would show up in Michigan, and most of them had years of prior experience— and he had never run the event before—decided to non-declare the POR In other words, his victory could not be counted in the final year-end standings! That decision cost him the 1977 SCCA National PRO Rally Championship.

Two weeks later Blok became lost, together with most of the field, on the final SCCA PRO Rally—The Mojave 24 Hour—and John Buffum was declared the 1977 SCCA champion.

Since Buffum had taken the SCCA national title away from Hendrik Blok, Blok repaid him in kind by winning the final NARRA event—The Mendocino Forest Rally in California—and taking Buffum's NARRA championship. Both 1976 national champions had repeated in 1977—but they had traded places.

It seemed an appropriate finish to the most competitive year yet to be experienced in professional rallying in the U.S.

So ended 1977—John Buffum's first year as a fully-sponsored factory rally driver. He had entered twenty rallies during the busy year and had won ten of them; three in a very tired Porsche, and seven in the new Triumph TR-7. He'd finished fourth on a world championship rally and he'd also won two of the three major North American championships. He was the runner-up in the Canadian National Championship, won by Taisto Heinonen, and his British Leyland sponsor finished second in both the U.S. and Canadian Manufacturer's Championships.

*9.4 JB and Vicki on stage in the Triumph TR-7 they drove to seven victories in 1977, winning both the SCAA PRO Rally National Championship and the SCCA/CASC North American Rally Cup Championship. It was their final year together.*

It was also a very good year for professional rallying in North America. The thirteen U.S. championship events presented by the SCCA and NARRA were won by eight different drivers. Triumph, Dodge, Porsche, Datsun, Plymouth, Volvo and Jeep had all taken overall victories in the U.S.

It was a hell of a year—but the best was yet to come.

*10.1 JB lets it all hang out in the David Sutton prepared Ford Escort at the 1978 Texaco Rallysprint (England). (Photo: Colin Taylor Productions)*

# 10
## Triple Crown
### Shoot-out In Wales

*1* 978 WAS AN EXCITING YEAR for professional rallying in North America as SCCA and NARRA each presented a ten-event series—twenty U.S. national championship rallies in a single season!

The ever hustling David Ash pulled off yet another promotional miracle, giving his NARRA organization a badly needed financial transfusion with national sponsorship from The Montgomery Ward Auto Club and the Porsche-Audi Division of Volkswagen of America. NARRA's America's Cup Championship was renamed the "Montgomery Ward Auto Club Challenge Cup Series."

Tom Grimshaw, NARRA's "National Promotion Director," was quoted in press releases welcoming MWAC and its one million members as sponsors of the '78 championship series. Until he happened to read one of the releases, Grimshaw had never heard the term "National Promotions Director." But not to worry, the following month Ash issued new press releases quoting him as NARRA's "National Publicity Director," and early in 1979, another press release dubbed him "NARRA's National Competition Director."

David Ash's promotional philosophy was, "You *can* fool most of the people most of the time."

To add icing to NARRA's cake, Ash announced the sanctioning of new events in Puerto Rico and Mexico.

John Buffum began the year with a co-driver change as Doug Shepherd, the young Chrysler engineer from Michigan, replaced Miss Vicki in the hot seat. The British Leyland-U.S. team also added Kleber Tires, Hella Lights and Bilstein Shocks to their sponsorship package.

Buffum's year was highlighted by seven events in England, including a special rally sprint shoot-out; hitting an ambulance in Puerto Rico; co-driving (and winning) with famed international driver, Stig Blomqvist; winning the Press On Regardless Rally (after eight previous tries); being disqualified from an FIA World Championship Rally; and putting it all together to become the first driver ever to win the triple crown of North American professional rallying—the SCCA National PRO Rally Championship, the NARRA National Championship, and the combined SCCA/CASC North American Rally Cup.

A good year—but not an easy one.

JB started by repeating his 1977 win of the Tri-State (TSD) Rally in the same stock TR-7 he'd used the previous year. It was his third Tri-State win in four years. The organizers added a new challenge to the '78 event by arranging for a twenty-three inch snowfall (blizzard).

SCCA's PRO Rally series started with a bang for both JB (defending SCCA champion) and Hendrik Blok (defending NARRA champion). Buffum began the first event, The Borax Bill Memorial in California City, Ca., in the same TR-7 he'd used in 1977. Blok introduced his new, very powerful, factory-backed Plymouth Arrow which was also financed by Mikuni (a Japanese carburetor company), and Kleber Tires.

Buffum's bang came from a rather easy win. Blok's came a mere half-mile into the opening spectator stage when he rolled the new Arrow several times, removing the co-driver's door, a portion of the windshield, and most of the right front fender. His encore, less then a mile later, was another roll which finished off the rest of the windows and his co-driver, Tom Grimshaw, who retired to the bar to await better days.

The Flying (upside down) Dutchman, slapped some new parts on the car, kidnapped a "volunteer" co-driver from the hotel lobby, and went on to finish fifteenth.

British Leyland sent a "new" used TR-7 to Libra Racing in February. It was the same car used by Marku Saaristo on the 1977 RAC Rally in England, and it made its debut in the U.S. with an 11.5-minute win for Buffum and Shepherd on the icy snow-packed roads of SCCA's 100 Acre Wood Rally in Missouri.

NARRA kicked its season off in March with the 24 Horas de Puerto Rico, starting and finishing in San Juan . . . .

**JB:** "After winning in Missouri we took the new car to NARRA's first '78 event in Puerto Rico. The San Juan Sports Car Club and Tourismo de Puerto Rico offered $400 starting money and free round trip vehicle transportation to the top fifteen NARRA points leaders based on their combined 1976-77 records.

It was a screwed up rally from the very start. The organizer's clocks were way off—sometimes as much as seven minutes in error. We had to walk into controls and look at their clocks to tell what time we should check in.

Blok brought his newest Plymouth Arrow over and blew his prop shaft a quarter-mile into the opening stage on the Caguas Raceway Circuit.

On Stage Four, which was run on the Salinas Army Base, we came around a sweeping right-hand bend and met a three-quarter-ton army ambulance head on. I tried to get across in front of it but we got hit on the right front hand corner at a 45-degree angle and totaled the car. The stage supposedly had been closed to all traffic an hour earlier.

111

The rally was such a mess the official scorer panicked and went home. The organizers asked Tom Grimshaw, Doug Shepherd and me to score the rally on Sunday morning. The first thing we did was eliminate any finisher who DNFed, according to the rules. It turned out that we eliminated every car that finished the rally. Everyone was so lost during the night that every team had exceeded the time bar. So we came up with our own set of rules and re-scored everything while people were howling outside the door in several languages. Finally we decided Bruno Kreibich and Scott Hughes from New York had won in a Baja VW, followed by Puerto Ricans, Carlos Ortiz and Francisco Torregrosa in a Subaru.

We never went back to Puerto Rico.**"**

**W**hile Buffum was crashing in Puerto Rico, British Leyland was releasing their hour-long television documentary, "Buffum & Co," in the U.S. As JB's reputation continued to grow in North America, he decided it was time to evaluate his driving against the big boys in Europe, where professional rallying was enjoying dramatic growth.

In April, Texaco sponsored a world-class rally sprint in Wales and John Buffum was invited to join fifteen international rally drivers in a "shoot-out" format which included no less than thirteen factory drivers in the starting list: Bjorn Waldegaard (Ford Escort RS), Billy Coleman (Lancia Stratos), Andy Dawson (Datsun Violet), Leif Asterhag (Toyota Celica), John Taylor (Escort RS), Tony Pond (Triumph TR-7), Hannu Mikkola (Escort RS), Stig Blomqvist (Saab Turbo), Timo Salonen (Fiat 131 Abarth), Brian Culcheth (Opel Kadette GTE), Pentti Arikkala (Vauxhall Chevette), Timo Makinen (Escort RS), and Russell Brookes (Escort RS).

John Buffum, in only his third year as a professional rally driver, was going head-to-head with the best in the world.

**JB:** "I was originally supposed to run a factory TR-7 in the Texaco Rally sprint, but there wasn't one available so I ended up in an Escort from David Sutton Cars, Ltd. of England.

During the practice runs I was third fastest behind Blomqvist and Mikkola, but I tried a bit too hard on the official three-mile downhill run and didn't make the first cut."

Russell Brooks set the pace on the first run with an average speed, **downhill**, in excess of 88 mph. After the second run it was down to Mikkola, Brookes, Blomqvist, and Pond. Mikkola and Pond won the third round and ran for the title.

Hannu Mikkola won by a margin of just over two seconds.

North American rally enthusiasts weren't disappointed with their champion's showing in Wales. It was enough that he was invited to join such an elite group and the fact that an American rally driver would be included in the BBC Television special could only help bolster rallying in North America.

Before returning to the states, JB completed his overseas trip with a great ninth place finish on the three-day Welsh Rally in a 2-liter Ford Escort with Glyn Roberts, a Manchester (England) bobby, reading instructions.

JB was to return to England four more times in 1978. He joined with Neil Wilson, an English co-driver who had been running with Brian Culcheth.

After DNFing their first rally, they did much better in their second outing, placing a factory Triumph TR-8 eighth overall on The Burmah Oil International in Scotland—a British Championship event. It was JB's first drive in the new Triumph TR-8—which was actually a TR-7 with a V-8 engine.

Later in the year, JB ran his own Escort on the Castrol-78 Rally.

*10.2 JB and Glyn Roberts finishing 9th on the 1978 International Welsh Rally in a Ford Escort. Note "USA" on both the windshield and hood, and American flags on front of the car. (Photo: Foster and Skeffington)*

**JB:** "I took John Brown on the Castrol-78 Rally in England. He was Russell Brookes' regular navigator but Brookes wasn't doing the event.

Brown was a real hard-ass.

We were on Dunlop A2 forest-racing tires and we kept having flats and weren't doing well overall. There was a twenty-mile stage through Hafren. Waldegaard and all the big names were there and we set the fastest time. At one point we were going along in fifth gear—like nine grand (9,000 rpm) in the Escort—and we're doing 110 mph. Then it got a bit slippy and I'm backing off just a little and Brown is yelling, 'Stay in it, stay in it, it's flat,' and I said, 'Jesus Christ, it's slippery!' He said to me, 'Look, I'm not telling you how to drive. I don't know what

114

the road condition is. I'm just telling you that the map says it is straight.'

Still, he was an excellent navigator and probably good for me because he pushed me all the time—but at 110 miles per hour in the mud, he seemed like a real dick. I took him with me again in November on the World Championship Lombard RAC International Rally which ran four days through Scotland and Wales and along the west coast of England.

Before the rally I did an auto show with my Ford Escort to promote the event and my sponsors, Spantape Services and Louver Curtains of England. They were giving away a free holiday in Spain to whoever guessed our finishing position on the RAC. We had planned on getting reporters inside the car but we lost the keys so I jumped on the hood with some cute little model and the rather conservative English press loved it and printed the photo in the newspapers the next day.

We DNFed the RAC with a bad alternator and a broken wheel. It was a cheap wheel . . . I was taking monetary shortcuts, which you sometimes have to do, but it always costs you in the end.**"**

Back in the U.S., following the Puerto Rico crash, Buffum's Libra Racing garage built a new lightweight red TR-7 with an aluminum roll cage . . . .

**JB:** **"**We took the new TR-7 to the second NARRA rally, The 20 Stages in Grayling, Michigan. British Leyland had shipped us a new motor but I didn't think it was running quite right so I decided to test it before the start.

I ran it just up to the red line and *poof*—it blew up. Later that night we were spectating and I met Rod Millen, the New Zealand rally champion who was over here for the first time, looking at U.S. rallying. We got drunk on our asses.**"**

115

The Old Fox, Scott Harvey, won the 20 Stages in his new one-off four-wheel-drive Dodge Aspen, taking an eight-second victory over Jim Walker's Volvo 142S. Defending NARRA champion, Hendrik Blok, blew the engine in his Plymouth Arrow and DNFed.

BL shipped yet another new 4-cylinder motor to Libra and Buffum used it to win his next two U.S. starts; the NARRA Olympus and the SCCA Susquehannock Trail.

Meanwhile, Libra Racing had built a new rally car for Saab-Scania U.S. earlier in the year and it was entered in the SCCA La Jornada Trabajosa Rally in California, with Stig Blomqvist driving and John Buffum co-driving! They won the rally by five minutes over Hendrik Blok.

Early the following year, Buffum bought the car from Saab and it is currently stored in his garage in Burlington, Vermont. It has one of the original 16-valve engines that were used in the first one-hundred models Saab homologated for FIA Group Two back in 1975.

A week later JB thanked Stig for his winning ride by beating him on the Baie des Chaleurs in Canada, where average speeds on stages exceeded 90 mph! It was not a nice way to treat a superstar from Sweden who had just given him a very relaxed winning ride in California, although, in all fairness, it must be noted that Blomqvist was driving a production Saab in Canada.

JB's '78 season was a series of wins, near wins, and violent crashes. He rolled his TR-7 in a garbage dump on the first stage of the Highlands Rally in Canada; was disqualified for running a stage without a helmet after he lost a wheel on the FIA International Criterium du Quebec; finished second in the old '77 Triumph with Vicki co-driving on the Canadian Lobster Rally; stuffed the same car off the road for a DNF on NARRA's HIS Rally; and won SCCA's POR (on his ninth try),

116

and NARRA's Chisum Trail Rally (Texas) and Northern Lights Rally (Michigan).

It was an up and down year but when it ended, John Buffum was both the SCCA and NARRA national champion and he took the North American Rally Cup for the third year in a row. In fact, until then he was the only driver who had ever won the NAR Cup since its inception in 1976. His primary sponsor, British Leyland, won NARRA's Manufacturer's Championship and placed second in SCCA's Manufacturer's Championship.

And . . . to underscore the fact that John Buffum was the dominant rally driver in North America, he had been invited to represent his country against the best in the world at the Texaco Rallysprint in Wales.

By the end of his fourth year as a full-time rally driver, John Buffum had already won thirty-four national championship events. . . and he was well on his way to a world record.

*11.1 John and Vicki with NARRA president, David Ash.*

# 11
## Out of Gas
### USA and NARRA

**A** MERICA, HOME OF THE BRAVE and land of the most wasteful society in the history of the world, suddenly discovered it could not buy a gallon of gasoline in 1979. The major oil producing countries formed a cartel known as OPEC and decided they could get more bucks for their bang by agreeing to reduce production, thereby creating a shortage which would drive prices upward on the world market. By July the price of a barrel of oil had jumped to $23.50. The following month it was up to $35 and still rising.

By mid-year Americans were shooting each other in gas stations. Nationwide, weekday traffic was down 8 percent, weekend traffic (when most stations closed) was down 20 percent; many states rationed gasoline on an odd-even system based on the last number on license plates and most stations wouldn't even pump gas into a tank that was more then half full.

Exxon, Mobil, Texaco and Standard of California posted the highest profit margins in their history and actor Marlon Brando summed up their position in his role as the leader of an American oil conglomerate in the movie titled *The Formula*. When an underling warned that the Arabs might keep raising prices, Brando replied, "You don't understand. We **are** the Arabs."

Unleaded gasoline rose to $1.87 if you pumped it yourself. The federally-dictated 55 mph national speed limit—designed to save both gasoline and lives—resulted in a 4 percent increase in traffic deaths, and for the first time in five years more than 50,000 Americans died on our "slower but safer highways."

When Lee Iacocca became the chairman of Chrysler we should have known our world's orbit had developed a slight kink and would never be the same again.

And, in 1979 John Buffum's total domination of professional rallying in North America was about to be seriously challenged.

Three-time New Zealand Rally Champion Rod Millen, moved to Newport Beach, California and formed an alliance with Mark Howard, a successful businessman who wanted to go rallying. Their Newport Rally Team began with a pair of Datsun 510s but in mid-season they switched to a very potent Mark II Ford Escort prepared in England by master builder, David Sutton.

Fiat introduced a new two-car team of Brava 131s, prepared by Abarth of Turin, Italy, and fully sponsored by Alitalia Airlines. Drivers, Jim Walker of Michigan and Dan Goodwin of Alaska would have 230-bhp and special rally crash boxes to support their drives for the U.S. championships.

Jon Woodner, a well-respected SCCA race driver, decided to turn his attention, and substantial private finances, to the rally scene and, with some guidance from Buffum, prepared to make his mark in a V-8 powered Triumph built in his own garage in Washington, D.C.

The Flying (often retired) Dutchman, Hendrik Blok, had a new and more powerful factory-backed Plymouth Arrow. He also had a new co-driver, Damon Trimble of California—his eighth in less than two years in the Mikuni-sponsored car.

120

Three-time Canadian national champion, Taisto Heinonen, perhaps the fastest of them all, decided the North American Rally Cup belonged in Canada and sported a new works Toyota Celica to back up his decision.

And what about defending champion John Buffum? He was starting the new season with a very tired 4-cylinder TR-7 and waiting for promised delivery of a new V-8 powered TR-8 (actually a beefed up TR-7). It wasn't going to be an easy year.

David Ash, the marketing munchkin from New York? He announced NARRA's signing of a new event—the Rally V de Guatemala. Until reading the press release, his competition committee had never heard of a rally in Guatemala, and, in fact, the event never did run under NARRA sanctioning.

The more things change the more they stayed the same! NARRA, acknowledging the oil crunch and requests from manufacturers, also introduced the first "Production Class" to U.S. stage rallying. The new class was designed to reduce costs by limiting elegibility to standard production vehicles sold in the US, and strictly limiting the modifications allowed on those basic models. The Canadian series had begun their production class the prior year and SCCA would follow suit in 1980.

When the bell sounded for the opening round of the SCCA series at The Big Bend Bash in Texas, everyone was expecting a real war between Buffum, Blok and Millen. Buffum won the opening two stages then retired with a broken oil line. Blok dropped back with a flat tire but came on strong and won the rally. Millen took a close second.

Buffum and Shepherd spent the evening in the Texas desert "mooning" people on the dusty stages. When they returned to their abandoned Triumph, which they had parked in the tiny village of Study Butte, they discovered that unknown parties had retaliated for their "over exposure." The TR-7 was completely filled with beer cans—empty ones, of course.

A surprise factory entry at The Bash was an International Harvester Scout II. Texan Dick Turner was giving the "farm truck" an experimental run to see if I.H. might want to become involved in the sport of stage rallying.

Turner finished first in Seed Four and sixth overall in a I.H. salesman's unprepared demo and immediately signed a two-year sponsorship deal with the factory.

Following Blok's opening victory, Buffum immediately answered back by winning the SCCA's 100 Acre Wood Rally in Missouri. It was JB's third consecutive win of the same rally—which was only three years old.

Blok took the lead in the SCCA point standings by finishing second, only forty-five seconds behind Buffum's TR-7.

As further proof that 1979 was going to be an interesting year, Kiwi Rod Millen won round three, the Tour de Forest in Washington. Blok and Taisto Heinonen finished second and third.

The top three finishers were separated by only forty-two seconds!

The Alitalia Fiat team made its debut at the Tour de Forest with a single car driven by Danny Goodwin. The Alaskan State trooper ran consistently in the top five until he hit a tree stump on Stage Six, sending his co-driver, Rod Sorenson, to the hospital with a cracked pelvis.

Buffum missed the Tour. He was in England, DNFing the Welsh Rally.

NARRA kicked its year off at the Olympus in Washington and Blok struck again when Buffum's Triumph blew a water hose, and Goodwin's Fiat blew tires and ended up high centered in a giant mud hole. Rod Millen became the first NARRA entrant to ever be time-barred because of arriving too early at a stage start control when Mark Howard, his co-driver and sponsor, made a slight miscalculation between Stages One and

122

Two and checked the Kiwi in twenty-five minutes early! Adios Rodney!

NARRA followed the successful Olympus with their Twenty Stages Rally which was forced to run two weeks earlier than

*11.2 Dan Goodwin/Rod Sorenson in the Alitalia Fiat 131 Brava, challenging a desert stage on the 1979 SCAA Nevada PRO Rally. (Photo: Su Kemper)*

planned because U.S. Forest Service rangers in Michigan did not want them to interfere with the mushroom picking season.

Millen lucked out by taking a seven-second win over Blok when the Flying Dutchman suffered a one-minute road penalty checking in early at a start control. Buffum's TR-7 blew a head gasket four stages from the finish, and Jim Walker celebrated his first drive in the Fiat 131 Abarth by finishing third overall.

And so it went, back and forth, throughout the year. Of the eleven SCCA championship rallies, Blok and Goodwin each won one, Taisto Heinonen won two, Buffum won three and Millen won four.

Of the eight NARRA events, Blok took one, Buffum took three, and Millen took the remaining four.

Buffum started slowly with the under-powered 4-cylinder TR-7, but the V-8 powered TR-8 finally arrived in time for him to post a win at NARRA's Chisum Trail Rally in Texas over Memorial Day weekend. JB finished the rally without a hood and with the oil cooler laying on top of the carburetors. Danny Goodwin put his Fiat in second place while Walker rolled his into a ball on Stage Six—which was titled "Walker's Run." Millen blew his transmission on the same stage.

At the SCCA's La Jornada Trabajosa rally in California, Fred Gallagher, a British Leyland factory co-driver from Scotland, joined JB in the old TR-7 to take first overall followed by Goodwin and Millen (who suffered three flats on stages). Blok would have finished third but he'd left his Fire Arrow's hood on Stage One and went back to retrieve it after the final stage—before starting the final seventy-mile transit to the finish in Bakersfield. He checked in twelve minutes late at the final control and dropped to sixth place.

Of course Hendrik protested everything—including every driver who drank a beer before starting the final transit (a longstanding tradition at the LJT, but one that was never repeated after 1979). When his protest was denied, Blok mailed his license to SCCA and quit rallying forever—again!

Shortly after his "forever" retirement, which lasted about two weeks, *Autoweek* featured an article on the volatile Dutchman which included a quote explaining his several crashes and rollovers, "You can't know how far you can go until you know how far too far is."

On the 24 Horas de Mexico, Shepherd took JB the wrong way on a transit between stages and caused him to finish both first and last. He was last in the total point standings for the event (because of the off-course excursion), but he was first on the stages after Danny Goodwin stuffed his Fiat while leading late in the rally. JB didn't get any of the $23,000 (U.S.) prize fund but he did get first place NARRA championship points since Ash, hearing that route instructions in Mexico were often incomplete or confusing, wisely decided only stage scores would be counted for NARRA finish positions.

Rod Millen had entered the Mexico event but never got his car across the border. Buffum sent his car over with Ken Adams, a long-time California rallyist who often competed in Mexico and fully understood the judicial use of cash donations (bribes) to Mexican officials. Millen's crew chief was refused entry at the California crossing because of his New Zealand citizenship—and because he failed to offer the proper tribute. He then tried to cross in Texas and ran into the same problem.

Finally, in desperation, the Kiwis attempted an illegal night crossing at a shallow point of the Rio Grande—the trailer got stuck and they returned to California.

In Canada, JB won the Piston les Wapitis Rally and might have been second on the Baie des Chaleurs except for a slight error in judgment. He decided to let his co-driver, Doug Shepherd, drive a stage and suggested that Shepherd first drive a transit to familiarize himself with the Triumph. They never reached the stage—Shepherd rolled the car on the transit!

Despite the fact that Walker and Goodwin were driving the best rally cars in the world—the Fiat 131 Abarth—they never did mount a serious challenge in either U.S. national series.

**JB:** "Here were two of the most experienced and quickest rally drivers in the U.S., driving excellent factory cars, and they never did anything with them—just like Bob Hourihan, who bought my 'Let's Boogie' Porsche and never placed it near the top of the standings. I think they showed us that it takes more than just a very good car—it also takes a very good driver to have a winning combination. Just because a driver is fast in an old slug does not necessarily mean he can transfer this skill and

125

be equally as good in a world class rally car. It takes a special combination of skill and equipment to be among the best. **"**

Jon Woodner spent the entire season unsuccessfully trying to sort out the change from pavement to gravel (racing to rallying) but did manage to place himself in the top five on three occasions. During the SCCA's Happiness Is Sunrise Rally in Pennsylvania, he spun his TR-8 so many times he lost count and finished with all four corners badly bent.

In October, Roy Donison of Gresham, Oregon, was killed in his production class Plymouth Fire Arrow when he had a head-on collision while tire testing in the mountains between rallies. It was never decided who was at fault—Donison or the driver of the large utility van that was said to be on the wrong side of the road, over a blind crest. He was posthumously awarded the first NARRA Production Class Championship and the following year, SCCA titled their Standard Production Class Championship, "The Donison Cup."

Bjorn Waldegaard of Sweden became the first World Champion Rally Driver as the FIA finally relented and created a championship for drivers. Until 1979, only manufacturers were awarded points on world championship rallies. Ford won the 1979 World Championship for Manufacturers.

"The Flying Finn," Taisto Heinonen, won the Canadian National Championship and reached his goal of taking the North American Rally Cup away from John Buffum (and the U.S.) by gleefully racing away from everyone on the ice-covered roads of Michigan's POR (November) and SnoDrift Rally (December).

John Buffum won the 1979 SCCA National PRO Rally Championship for the third year in a row. It was the fourth time he'd won the SCCA national title during his five years of competition.

Rod Millen and Hendrik Blok finished second and third respectively in the SCCA championships, but Millen took the

*11.3 JB on the 1979 RAC World Championship Rally—driving one of five factory-entered Triumph TR-8s. (Photo: Foster and Skeffington, Ltd.)*

NARRA National Rally Championship in his first year of U.S. competition. Buffum and Blok finished second and third.

JB also returned to England in November to have another go at the Lombard RAC World Championship Rally. British Leyland entered five bright red TR-8s in the 1979 RAC. Two were driven by Scandinavians, two by British drivers, and one by American, John Buffum. Midway through the first night observers were amazed to learn that Buffum was leading all the other Triumph factory drivers—but later he slid off the road in Kielder Forest and DNFed.

Despite his non-finish, British rally enthusiasts would remember John Buffum—the rather crazy but very quick American driver—in the British car powered by an American V-8.

127

It was an exciting and hard-fought year. It was another national championship year for John Buffum . . . and, although we didn't yet know, it was to be the final curtain for David Ash and NARRA.

1969 Monte Carlo Rallye. Bjorn Waldegard stands triumphant, holding aloft the winner's cup in front of Prince Rainier and Princess Grace Kelly.

JB practicing in the 3-Liter CSL BMW that the Hurtig Team Libra used in the 1974 IMSA Camel GT Series.

Jean-Paul Perruse and John Bellefleur landing the Fiat 124 Spyder on the 1974 Rally of the Rideau Lakes WCR (Canada).

Canadian champion, Taisto Heinonen, and co-driver Tom Burgess, slip sliding away on a snow-covered stage in their factory sponsored Toyota Celica.

JB and Vicki avoiding the trees on their way to victory in the 1976 Northern Lites Rally (Michigan) in the ex-works Porsche 911 they purchased from Polish National Champion, Sobieslaw Zasada. (Photo: Matt Jerue)

The "stars" in David Ash's NARA star system. John and Vicki in the Stars & Stripes Bicentennial Special Ford Escort. (Photo: Matt Jerue)

The John & Vicki Show boogeying down a stage on the 1976 Lombard RAC
World Championship Rally (England), in their right-hand drive Ford Escort RS
1600. (Photo: Foster and Skeffington)

JB, showing English co-driver, Glyn Roberts, how to take a Mark II Ford Escort
through a tight left on the 1978 Welsh Rally. (Photo: Foster & Skeffington)

*P-4*

JB and Doug Shepherd washing the '79 Triumph TR-8 on stage. (Photo: Tim Cline)

JB and Neil Wilson in their Darth Vader helmets, trying to get their Triumph TR-8 through Kielder Forest on the 1980 Lombard RAC WCR. They survived Kielder but not the rally—DNF. (Photo: Motofoto Sports Photography)

JB celebrating in the saddle of a Pony Express rider's horse after winning the 1983 Carson City International PRO Rally.

JB, with Neil Wilson, in the works prepared Talbot Sunbeam Lotus showing an ambulance crew the fine art of cornering in the dirt on the 1982 Costa Smeralda Rally in Sicily.

Getting a bit of sun while practicing for the '83 Pikes Peak Auto Hill Climb. Left to right: Audi's, Mike Rossman, JB, and his service crew: "Salty" Sottolano and John Beauvais.

Team Libra International—1983 SCCA National PRO Rally Champions. Left to right: John Beauvais, "Salty" Sottolano, Doug Shepherd, and John Buffum—standing before the Nevada State Capitol Building in Carson City.

"I took my helmet to Germany and brought my helmet home. Just another day's work." JB and Arwed Fischer winning the 1983 Sachs Winter Rally in Germany.

The morning the "rally" cars went "racing," following JB's victory on the 1984 Oregon Trail PRO Rally. Left to right: Rod Millen (4WD Mazda RX-7), John Buffum (Audi Quattro), Steve Millen (4WD Mazda RX-7), Rear—Jon Woodner (Peugeot).

JB and Neil Wilson holding the Audi Quattro in third place, behind Ari Vatanen and Hannu Mikkola, on the final day of the 1984 Lombard RAC Rally (England). Photo was taken just before their accident on Stage 40. (Photo: Motofoto Sports Photography)

The only American driver to ever win a European Championship Rally: Fred Gallagher (r) and John Buffum, first overall on the 1984 Cyprus Rally. "Now it feels great!" (Photo: Nikos Mitsouras)

Fred Gallagher and JB wait to start the 1984 Acropolis World Championship
Rally in Lagonisi, Greece. Note the word "Tires" added to the BFGoodrich decal
on the fender—just to let the foreign press know what BFGoodrich had provided
for the team. (Photo: Nikos Mitsouras)

Buffum and Neil Wilson flogging the Group A Coupe Quattro through a stage of the 1987 Olympus World Championship Rally before the serious crash that sent them sight-seeing to Mount Ranier National Park with several DNFed teams.

Kiwi, Rod Millen's beautifully prepared and very potent one-off—4WD Mazda RX-7. (Photo: Su Kemper)

1987—The Perfect Year! JB and Tom Grimshaw in the "Killer Bee" Sport Quattro. (Photo: Nikos Mitsouras)

Buffum and Gallagher on one of the very rough stages of the 1984 Acropolis WCR (Greece). (Photo: Nikos Mitsouras)

John and Mary Buffum and children (L to R) Michelle, Paul, and Julie.

The very fast, but a bit crazy American, about to start the '84 Acropolis Rally in Greece.

JB and Fred Gallagher picking up the gold in Cyprus, 1984. (Photo: Nikos Mitsouras)

JB waits for the start flag at the 31st Acropolis Rally, 1984. (Photo: Nikos Mitsouras)

1973 POR (Michigan): The opening spectator stage on Belle Isle. JB and Vicki in the Libra Ford Escort. (Photo: Gero Hoschek)

Tom Grimshaw (L), John Buffum and Jeff Andretti (R), pose atop the Audi they drove to victory in the 1987 One Lap of America—an event Buffum has won five times.

# 12
## End of the Line
### Buffum's Firebreak

A MERICAN SPORTS FANS will remember 1980 as "The Year of the Miracle," when a bunch of brash kids from the U.S. beat the invincible Russian hockey team, to take the gold at the winter Olympics.

North American rally fans will remember several things about 1980: The death of NARRA, The Golden West (Worst?) 2000, the one-million-dollar team sponsorship deal, and the tie for the national championship going into the final event, one week before Christmas.

At NARRA's annual convention in Chicago, members of Ash's "competition committee" decided they were tired of looking like fools because of his promotional theatrics, which included published event calendars listing rallies that never happened; promises of inflated prize funds that never materialized; unpaid bills, and large amounts of dollars many believed were finding their way into Ash's pocket.

The competition committee didn't really care if David Ash was getting rich (which was highly unlikely) off his NARRA organization. What they wanted was a solid schedule and a guaranteed amount of financial support for their 1980 events.

Faced with open rebellion, Ash relented. He established five "Super Rallies" for 1980 and guaranteed a $7,500 prize fund for each event—$35,000 for the 1980 season. Ash concluded the Chicago meeting with the announcement that the Montgomery Ward Auto Club would not be a sponsor in 1980 but, not to worry, the entire series would be sponsored by Volkswagen of America.

Press announcements went out, everybody was happy, and NARRA's future was guaranteed—until the first event.

The Golden West 2000, the first "Super Rally," was to run May 7 to May 11. It was to start and finish in San Francisco and included overnight halts in Reno, Nevada.

A NARRA press release, issued two weeks prior to the start, expanded the guaranteed prize fund from $7,500 to $50,000!

Even more excitement was generated by the news that BFGoodrich Tire Company would produce a film titled *Rally: A Race Against Time* at the Golden West 2000. BFG had just recently entered the sport and were already providing tires and financial assistance to several teams—including those of John Buffum and Rod Millen.

Camera crews began pre-filming with several teams the week prior to the start of the GW-2000. The teams were issued their start numbers and NARRA/VWOA sponsor decals early to assure the pre-filming would look like legitimate rally action.

The brown stuff hit the fan the day prior to the start when NARRA's support check bounced, and things turned truly ugly when Ash suddenly announced that the Montgomery Ward Auto Club had changed its mind and would indeed sponsor the 1980 series—and the rally cars would be required to display over-sized MWAC decals—which he just happened to have in his luggage.

The event organizers refused to allow the new decals which would nullify all the expensive work already completed by the BFGoodrich film crews.

The Golden West 2000 began the following morning with

130

David Ash moving down the starting line plastering MWAC decals on the rally cars, and drivers jumping out to remove them.

Midway through the second day Ash posted a notice at a meal halt proclaiming the rally to be canceled, the event insurance coverage to be nullified, and further stating that any rallyist restarting the event would forfeit their license forever!

Tom Grimshaw, NARRA competition director, personally tore up the notice, jumped into his I.H. Scout with driver, Dick Turner, and led the restart out of town.

Ash attempted to keep NARRA alive for a few more months and did present one more small event—but he was beating a dead horse. The North America Rally Racing Association was no more.

Still, it must be said that David Ash was undoubtedly the best thing that ever happened to professional rallying in the U.S., not only because he helped the sport emerge from the shadows, but because he taught all—organizers and competitors alike—the importance of public relations, publicity, and sponsorship. He also attracted media attention to the sport by creating a situation between two factions—NARRA and SCCA— that demonstrated the American ideals of free enterprise: "Competition breeds growth."

Of course, in the long run, he was doomed to failure because professional rallying in the U.S. was not big enough to support two national championship series. But in the short term, he did force the SCCA to wake up and compete. He proved to them for several years that they were not necessarily "the only show in town."

The Golden West 2000, which became known as the "Golden Worst," was a terrible rally, but a great adventure. It included stages in excess of one hundred miles in length. One 125-mile stage included a fuel pit stop in the middle of the Nevada desert with the time included in the total stage score.

131

A ninety-mile desert stage had a single instruction: "Left at the dead cow"—and there was indeed a dead cow lying alongside the road. There was also a service stop at a Nevada whorehouse in the middle of the desert.

The rally was won by two newcomers from New Zealand, John Woolf and Grant Whitakker, in a Mazda RX-3. Millen lost the rally when an incorrect instruction left service crews lost in the desert eight miles from the service area listed in competitor's route books. Some service crews found their teams—Millen's did not, and he was forced to motor slowly through the following 125-mile stage to stretch fuel consumption until he could reach the mid-point "pit stop."

Several teams dropped out of contention when they

12.1 1980: JB and Doug Shepherd leave Alcatraz behind as they start the Golden West 2000 (the rally that signaled the end of NARRA) in San Francisco. (Photo: John G. Rettie)

132

became stuck in a very deep sand wash and had to join forces to free their cars one by one. Buffum avoided the problem when he drove up a bank, landed on the elevated hardpan, kept full throttle on for a hundred yards and popped back down onto the road, past the point of the melee. That instantaneous decision saved him for the moment but he too lost the rally when he bent the steering rack, broke the suspension and lost several pieces off his TR-8 as the result of bashing a very deep washout at high speed.

It was only the first week in May and already the 1980 season was showing signs of being the strangest year of them all.

It got even stranger in October at the SCCA's Big Bend Bash rally in Texas when the awards banquet was interrupted so everyone could watch good ol' boy, Dick Turner sign a one-million-dollar sponsorship contract with LubriLon, a Texas Corporation peddling a synthetic oil additive.

LubriLon actually paid the team about $25,000 the following year before hitting the financial skids. With NARRA fading into the history books, the SCCA National PRO Rally Championship gained in stature because it finally was the only show in town. With several NARRA rallies switching back to the SCCA series, competitors now had a full thirteen-event schedule to whet their appetites.

Buffum started the year on a high note, winning the first two events—the 100 Acre Wood in Missouri and the Tour de Forest in Washington. But Millen stayed close, taking second place on both events in his new, and very quick Mazda RX-7.

Hendrik Blok appeared at the 100 Acre Wood with a new ultra-light Mazda GLC powered by a rotary engine. Shortly after the start of the opening stage, a large fire appeared between co-driver Rod Sorenson's legs and the "Super Glick" burst into flames. This strange adventure was repeated at the Olympus Rally in Washington when the GLC again caught fire

133

fifty feet from the start line of the first stage. Blok and Sorenson dove out of the car, put the fire out, jumped back in, buckled up, and motored on.

Jon Woodner was finally learning how to keep his TR-8 from spinning like a top and finished third in Missouri. Before the end of the '80 season he would post two seconds, two thirds and a fourth—the racer was becoming a rallyist.

Millen took the Olympus Rally when Buffum stuffed his Triumph into the woods for a DNF, but JB retaliated with a win at Michigan's Northern Lights Rally while the quick Kiwi stayed home to rebuild his car. Then Buffum did it again in Texas at the Chisum Trail Rally and the new Kiwis, Woolf and Whittaker, followed him home in second place.

John Woolf and Grant Whittaker had rallied together since they were sixteen years old in New Zealand. When rally experts were discussing the 1980 season, before it began, nobody had even heard their names in North America. They made their first appearance at the GW-2000—and won. They came to Texas and finished second. Then they went to Pennsylvania and won the Susquehannock Rally. They followed up with a second on the La Jornada Trabajosa—just ten seconds behind Millen! When their first year was over John Woolf finished third in the national driver's championship and Grant Whittaker finished second, behind Doug Shepherd, in the national co-driver's standings.

These guys had come to the U.S. to play hardball!

All the Mazdas broke in Pennsylvania and Buffum posted his fifth and final U.S. win for 1980 at the Happiness Is Sunrise Rally. At that point he had Rodney Millen by the throat and could slow down a bit.

Perhaps he slowed down too much, or perhaps he had more important matters in mind. In October he married Mary Choiniere, the ex-wife of his former business partner, Paul

134

Choiniere, and acquired an instant family with two stepchildren, Michelle and Paul, Jr.

Regardless the reason, Millen came on to win the next three events in a row—the Mendocino Forest Rally in California, Big Bend Bash in Texas, and Press On Regardless in Michigan.

At the POR Buffum had what he calls a "B-I-I-I-G moment" when he hit a tree and totaled his TR-8 . . . .

**JB:** "We came over a rise on Barker Lake Road and the road went about 20 degrees to the right although it looked like it went maybe only 5 degrees to the left through a break in the trees. As soon as I saw where the road really went, I knew we were going to go off, and in about the last instant, I remember thinking *I could get hurt*. We were flat out in fourth gear and hardly slowed down at all before we hit.

I braced myself and closed my eyes. We hit, and everything stopped. I opened my eyes and looked around. The dash was all messed up, and the steering wheel was way over to the right. Doug and I looked at each other and said, 'Are you all right?'

I reached up and shut off the ignition, and then I shut off the lights  Then I felt this pain in my foot. Wow! My right foot was trapped between the transmission tunnel and the brake pedal, and my left foot was wedged next to it. God it hurt!

I yelled at Doug to get the winch or something to pull the brake pedal off my foot. I guess I got pretty excited. I started thrashing around and yelling at Doug to do something. Then I reached down and found out I could move the pedal to the left just enough to move my foot.

Then I really started getting cold and Doug got me about three jackets. I put one on and used the others to cover myself and sat there and shivered. Doug set out a warning triangle and ran to the finish control which was about a mile away. Turner was at the finish control and he drove his Scout through the woods to get back to me but by the time he got there I was already out of the car and limping around.**"**

T he firebreak John Buffum momentarily mistook for the main road became known as "Buffum's Firebreak" from that night on. Tim Cline wrote of the accident in *Autoweek* . . .
"It's 10 A.M. on a cold overcast Saturday in Michigan's Upper Peninsula. The most gifted professional rally driver in America does not look the part. He is walking down Shelten Avenue in downtown Houghton—slowly, gingerly, like an old man . . . . What do you think about, sitting there all alone, shivering in the cold? Buffum does not come out and say it, but it's clear in the tone of his voice and the look in his eyes— even the front runners are vulnerable when pitted against the elements in what is considered America's toughest auto rally."

Fortunately Buffum's injuries were not as serious as he first thought and he left immediately for England to drive a factory TR-8 on the Lombard RAC Rally.Tim Cline also covered the RAC for *Autoweek*, and wrote:
"American John Buffum, in one of the factory TR-8s, overcame all manner of trouble, including spins and a thirty-minute off-course excursion in the Kielder Forest, to climb to fifteenth place only to have the whole thing dissolve when the car's rear axle let go on the last of the rally's seventy special stages, less than seven miles from the end of the rally."
A twenty-four-year-old Finn, Henri Toivinen, won the RAC in a Talbot Sunbeam Lotus and became the youngest driver to ever win one of the most important championship rallies in the entire world.

A short time later, JB was back in Michigan starting the SnoDrift Rally with the same Triumph he drove in England. The factory air-shipped the car to the U.S. as a replacement for the TR-8 he'd written off at the POR.

The SnoDrift featured a fourteen-inch snowfall, freezing rain, and fog so thick the weather bureau issued a traveler's advisory. JB stuffed his TR-8 into a snowbank early on and lost a lot of time digging out. Then Millen's navigator took him off course in the thick fog and Guy Light, a Michigan driver in a Jeep CJ-7, took the win.

Buffum actually beat Light but lost the rally when, after passing the Michigan driver on a stage, he arrived at a finish line only to find the control personnel sound asleep! If that stage had been scored, Buffum would have won and broken the year-end tie with Rod Millen before they went to the final rally in Nevada. As it was, the Kiwi had a slight edge on Buffum because of SCCA's tie-breaking rules. But it would all come down to the last rally of 1980.

The final duel in Nevada, the week before Christmas, would decide the 1980 national championships. Every North American rally driver of note was entered in the Frontier Hotel/Casino Nevada Rally and, as expected, the battle would come down to Buffum, Millen, Blok, Heinonen, and Woolf— with off-road racing super star, Ivan Stewart, and several other heavy hitters waiting in the wings.

Not only was the national championship on the line, everyone was eager to get a share of the $20,000 prize fund to be paid in leather pouches full of silver dollars—the richest payout in the history of professional rallying in the United States.

Millen opened with a win on the first twenty-one mile stage across a dry lake-bed and over a low mountain. Then Taisto Heinonen took the next stage by two seconds over

Buffum. Buffum suffered a flat on a stage and fell back but Ivan Stewart was staying close to the leaders, and by the lunch break on the first day the order was Millen, Heinonen, Buffum and Stewart.

At that point JB gave up all hope of winning another national championship. His car was acting sickly and Millen was moving away from him on every stage.

Later that same night, Millen's RX-7 was screaming down a long straight towards a brightly lighted finish control. Millen could see the control, but did not see a gentle jog around a sandpile—a jog he had passed just two hours earlier going the other way. Millen hit the dirt at 120 mph and launched the Mazda twenty feet into the air. It came down on its tail, cartwheeled into a dry wash and landed upside down. Millen and his co-driver, Mike Franchi, escaped with minor bruises, but their rally was over.

**JB:** "Rod Millen seemed to suffer from the same problem I used to have to deal with—he didn't know when to slow down. He had more than a three-minute lead and a guaranteed national championship—and he was still going just as fast as he was at the start of the rally.

In Nevada this problem cost him the national championship."

A short time later, Ivan Stewart's navigator made a timing mistake and checked into a closed *parc ferme* thirty minutes late. Stewart, ever the gentleman, thanked the organizers for a very good event but declined to start at the back of the pack the next day, and withdrew.

Buffum's Triumph was ailing with a sick carburetor when he restarted the second day and Millen waited at the final finish control to see if the Triumph would come through. He stood on a railroad bridge, alone in the dark, as Taisto Heinonen's 16-valve Toyota Corolla crossed the finish line in a cloud of desert dust to take first overall. Then he saw Buffum's TR-8 limping home in second place and knew his championship hopes were gone. Millen immediately got into a car and drove home to California, skipping the awards banquet.

With his second place finish on the final rally of the year, John Buffum became the SCCA National PRO Rally driving champion for 1980. He also won the Manufacturer's Championship for his sponsor, Jaguar Rover Triumph, Inc., and by virtue of his four wins in Canada during the year, he captured his fourth North American Rally Cup.

It was also his final North American appearance in a Triumph . . . .

**JB:** "At the end of 1980 I could see the handwriting on the wall. I knew Triumph wasn't building any more cars and Mike Cook was hinting that they might not come back in 1981. Finally, in December, he told me they were not going to return and my ride was over.

I had four good years with Triumph. We ran two 4-cylinder TR-7s and two 8-cylinder TR-8s and won a lot of rallies and a lot of championships."

It was a good ride . . . but it was the end of the line.

139

*12.2 1980 POR: The results of "Buffum's Firebreak." (Photo: Matt Jerve)*

# PART THREE

*JB and Tom Grimshaw entertaining the spectators with the Group B Audi Sport Quattro on the opening stage of the 1987 Sunriser Forest Rally in Ohio. (Photo: Robert A. Griffith)*

# 13

# Vorsprung Durch Technik
## A Hot Rod Lincoln In Lederhosen

*I*N THE FALL OF 1980 devotees of professional rallying were given a hint of the startling world-wide revolution that
was about to change the face of the sport and the high
performance automotive market, forever. John Watson wrote
his recollections in England's *Autosport* magazine:

"First impressions, as they wheeled the Audi Quattro
Turbo Coupe on to the grass at the Balaia Hotel on the
Algarve coast of Portugal, were certainly deceiving. It was
October 1980, the launch of the German rally campaign
and, while Hannu Mikkola added credibility, having developed the four-wheel-drive prototype in front of us, the car
looked cumbersome, not at all a sleek new rally racer for
the future. One day later, in a rally environment of gravel
roads winding through the mountains which provide the
backdrop to the Algarve beaches, the potential was more
readily demonstrated.

"Vorsprung Durch Technik (Progress Through Technology)—emblazoned on the support trucks even at this
stage of the project—would soon be forcing the cynics to
think again. Using the Quattro to open the course, Mikkola
'beat' the winning car by over nine minutes!"

The Quattro Turbo Coupe was initially designed as a
luxury autobahn touring car, or as Jay Lamm described it in his

*All-Wheel-Drive High-Performance Handbook,* "It was sort of a hot rod Lincoln in lederhosen."

Only a handful of people in North America were aware of Audi's program to develop a four-wheel-drive automobile and even fewer were aware that the Ingolstadt engineers believed rallying would provide the perfect arena for launching their revolution.

John Buffum was one of those few who immediately realized the future potential of Audi's new rally program.

**JB:** "When the 1980 season ended I didn't know what I was going to do. I'd been in professional rallying for six years, had fifty wins on national championship events, won the U.S. National Rally Championship each of the six years (five SCCA titles and one NARA title), and I'd taken four North American Rally Cup Championships . . . but I didn't have a ride for 1981.

There weren't a lot of possibilities available in the U.S. at that time.

In February, out of the blue I got a telephone call from Larry Edwardes with Peugeot. He asked if I wanted to drive a factory-prepared Peugeot 504 V-6 Coupe in the opening event in Texas. The car had done the East African Safari. So I said, 'Sure, absolutely.' Then he asked if I wanted to sign with Peugeot for the entire year, and I said I would do the one rally and see how it went.

The reason I did not want to commit to a full season was that back in 1980 I'd been reading about a new Audi rally program in Europe and I wondered if they'd do anything in the U.S.

Josef Hoppen was in charge of the competition department of Porsche-Audi U.S., and I knew he was interested in rallying because his company backed the NARRA championship series before it self-destructed.

144

So I had talked to Bill Oursler, Hoppen's public relations man, at the end of the 1980 HIS Rally, and asked him what he thought Audi was going to do. He said no one knew for sure, yet.

(We called Oursler 'The Duck,' because he walked like one, and every time he waddled by you could hear someone saying, 'quack, quack, quack' behind his back.)

By February I still hadn't heard from Oursler or Hoppen so I took the Peugeot ride on The Big Bend Bash PRO Rally."

Anyone with the foresight to bet that John Buffum, the defending national champion and dominant professional rally driver in North America, would only win a single event in 1981, could have made a lot of money, because that is exactly what happened.

New Zealander, Rod Millen, who lost the 1980 national championship to JB by a single mistake on the final event of the season, was determined to reverse his fortunes in 1981 with a new, meticulously prepared, Mazda RX-7, modified by "lots of little changes we learned from last year."

The Mazda factory also added a second team car for the '81 season. It was manned by two other Kiwis, John Woolf and Grant Whittaker, the boys who had won the Golden West 2000—the first rally they'd ever entered in the U.S.

Dick Turner was back with a lighter soft top I.H. Scout, and a new engine—a 540 hp V-8 monster!

Ron Clyborne, a wealthy newcomer from West Virginia, purchased both of the ill-fated factory Fiat 131 Abarths previously driven by Walker and Goodwin, and was determined to make a serious run at the U.S. title. Clyborne had been very successful in off-road racing and intended to spend whatever it took to be just as successful in professional rallying.

145

Jon Woodner slipped a very powerful Ford BDA engine in a Datsun and figured to be among the front runners at every rally.

And, to add to the excitement of the new season, BFGoodrich Tire Company made a serious commitment to the sport by signing sponsorship deals with most of the top pro teams and backing them at every event with a very handsome, fully-equipped, 18-wheel service truck.

The news that industry giants, such as Budweiser, were going to sponsor some major events, indicated that professional rallying in North American was continuing to grow.

Buffum's 1981 defense of his national title began and ended on the rough desert roads of the Terlinqua Ranch in Texas' Big Bend country.

**JB:** "The Peugeot 504 we used in Texas was set up for African Safari Rally specs. It was cumbersome but easy to handle. Peugeot also sent over a works mechanic who could speak no English. Fortunately I could speak enough French to carry on a conversation with him.

Jean-Pierre Nicolas had used the car on the African Safari and when we got it, it had two clips mounted on the transmission tunnel. I asked the mechanic what they were for and he said, 'For the hammer.' I couldn't imagine why anyone would carry a hammer mounted inside the car but he explained that Jean-Pierre dreaded going off the road and being trapped inside the car, so he carried a big hammer to beat out the windows so he could free himself.

The car came with four semi-used Michelin rally tires. We only had three sets of BFGoodrich Comp T/As for the Big Bend so we took the Michelins with us. That decision caused a rift between Rod Millen and me that lasted for several years.

We used one set of BFGs during practice and went through the other two sets during the daylight sections on the rocky

146

Terlinqua Ranch roads. So when we came off the ranch and got ready for the night section, we drove off course, met our service crew, and mounted the Michelins.

At that point Millen and I were about fifteen seconds apart. But then I went on to win the night section and took the rally by about a minute and a half over Millen and Dick Turner.

During the final long transit to the finish, we met our service crew again and changed back to BFG tires since they were one of our major sponsors. Millen noticed our tire change and had a mechanic take a Polaroid picture of the Peugeot with the Michelins on. At the finish he was really pissed off and started raising hell about our tire change, despite the fact we had violated no rules.

Since both he and I were sponsored by BFGoodrich I think he was trying to cause me some embarrassment by complaining to the BFG reps, the press, the officials, everyone who would listen.

But the BFG guys didn't want to hear about it. I carried their decals on the car, used their tires at the start and through most of the rally, and had them on at the finish. As far as the public and press were concerned, I'd won the rally on BFGoodrich Comp T/As. But I thought Millen's conduct was very unprofessional, or perhaps just a case of sour grapes.

Of course there was usually a bit of tension between Millen and I since he and I battled each other, well in front of the rest of the field, for many years. We were each other's main competition so there was bound to be a certain amount of low-level hostility. We watched each other pretty closely.

Most of us in this sport go out of our way to help each other. We have to rely on each other because if something goes wrong in the woods we're the first ones on the scene and the first ones able to help in an emergency. So Millen's behavior was certainly out of character for our sport. **"**

Millen avenged the opening loss with a win in Missouri on the 100 Acre Wood Rally—an event JB had won four previous times. Buffum returned with the Peugeot but lost the rally on the final stage when he blew a tire in a culvert and settled for second place.

*13.1 JB and Doug Shepherd making dust while practicing for the 1981 Big Bend Bash PRO Rally on the Terlinqua Ranch roads in Texas. Note the original Michelin decals on the hood of the Peugeot 504 V-6 Coupe. They were changed to BFGoodrich before the start.*

However, if the rules of *force majeure* had been properly applied by the organizers, JB would have won his fifth 100 Acre Wood Rally.

**JB:** "Missouri was another very close battle between Millen and me. Late in the night we ran a stage that had been opened by the course opening car. It included a gooey swampy section that I just chugged through in first gear, but Millen stuck his Mazda behind me and blocked the course. Dick Turner got around him in his Scout but stopped to tow him out along with several following cars that also got stuck.

When we finished the stage we went to a service area for about twenty minutes and no one showed up while we were there. In fact, when we left for the next set of stages, no cars had arrived at the service area and we figured they had all exceeded the thirty-minute time bar and were disqualified. We thought we'd won the rally at that point. The rules of *force majeure* in professional rallying say that once the course opening car has gone through and the stage is open for competition, it is the competitor's duty to complete it—except in the case of a medical emergency.

But the organizers and SCCA steward decided differently. They could have extended the time bar period and let all the cars continue on the rally—but they would have a large time penalty because of the pile up in the woods. Instead they decided to scrub the stage—drop it from the scoring, and Millen was back in the game and beat us when we had a problem on the final stage.

There was also another factor that may or may not have colored their decision. It was only the fifth year for the 100 Acre Wood Rally and I'd won all of them until 1981. Doug Shepherd and I discussed the possibility that the organizers may have made their ruling because they wanted to see a new name and new car in the list of past winners. Stranger things have happened.**"**

The Missouri rally was to be JB's final drive for Peugeot . . . .

**JB:** "Finally I had to make a decision. The Peugeot, at that time, was a far better car than a two-wheel drive Audi, and I could have had it for the entire season, but in March I met with Jo Hoppen in New Jersey and we discussed a rally program.

149

Then Bill Oursler called and asked me to write Hoppen a letter saying I'd like to do six or eight events and I wanted a car and $20,000 or so. Hoppen said OK, and I switched to Audi.

We got two ex-works Audi 4000s (Audi 80 in Europe). They were front wheel drive, 4-cylinder, 160 HP, and, although it was probably the best handling rally car I ever drove, it soon became clear we did not have enough power to stay with the top guys. **"**

**B**uffum's switch to Audi did not end his association with Peugeot as his Libra Racing organization was contracted to manage the Peugeot effort for the balance of the '81 season. JB hired his long time Canadian adversary, and friend, Jean Paul Perusse, and co-driver John Grimshaw, to campaign the 504. He also hired a second full time service mechanic, John Beauvais, to assist Salty Sottolano in maintaining the three factory cars.

JB introduced the Audi 4000 in his usual "Stuffum" fashion, rolling the new car on a press stage before the start of the Olympus PRO Rally in Washington. Once again his service crew worked throughout the night and had the car ready to take the start flag the following morning.

He finished third, behind Millen and Taisto Heinonen.

The Olympus was a portent of things to come.

In Michigan, Buffum and Shepherd DNFed with a holed piston. In Texas they finished third because a stage that would have given them a victory over Millen's Mazda, was canceled when a tornado wiped out all timing records, control boards and much of the surrounding forest. The same storm took fifteen lives in Northern Texas.

In Pennsylvania the Audi jumped out of gear and the resulting spin off the road relegated him to second place.

It was that kind of a year . . . .

150

**JB:** "We finally convinced Audi we needed more power and they sent us a new (used) five-cylinder car. It had Quattro suspension and some other stuff we tried a few times, but we still couldn't win in it.

The first rally with the new five cylinder engine was The Centennial in Colorado . . . we broke a drive shaft. Then we finished third on the Tour de Forest in Washington because of a broken brake caliper, and DNFed the Sunriser in Ohio with another broken drive shaft.

It took us two rallies to realize there was no steering lock in the car and the steering was turning at too much of an angle. It was a factory-prepared rally car and we just never thought about it, but that's why I had such a hell of a time driving it at first.

I was still gambling on getting a Quattro and at the POR we put a sticker on the rear window that read, 'All I want for Christmas is a Quattro.' We caught Woodner on a stage at the POR, in deep snow, which slowed us down, but it didn't matter because I stuffed us off for another DNF. We finished the season with a hole in the block for a DNF on the Reno International Rally.

It was a frustrating year."

**R**od Millen won the SCCA National PRO Rally Championship in 1981. He also won the manufacturer's championship for Mazda of North America. Canadian, Taisto Heinonen, took his second North American Rally Cup Championship.

John Buffum did not compete in Canada in 1981 and thus did not qualify for the North American Rally Cup, but he did manage to fit eight overseas rallies into his busy schedule. BFGoodrich sponsored his European tour and he ran the same Triumph TR-8 he'd used on the '80 RAC Rally. The car had

151

been shipped to the U.S. for the final 1980 championship event in Nevada, then returned to England for refitting by Pete Harrison Rally Preparation, Ltd. of Wolverhampton (near Birmingham) before start of the '81 season.

JB's "European Adventure," as he called it, also had financial backing from Hella (lighting) of Germany and technical assistance from British Leyland.

His best finish was a second on the Tour of Cumbria. He finished seventh on the West Park Welsh Rally in Wales, eighth on the Haspengouw in Belgium, rolled on the Scottish Rally, broke a half shaft on the 24 Hours of Ypres in Belgium, crashed on the Hunsruck in Germany, broke a transmission on the Limburgia Rally in Holland, and DNFed the RAC Rally in England with a broken block.

Despite the apparent non-success of his "adventure," JB's performance was remarkable for two reasons: (l) He was the first American driver to ever mount a serious challenge in the highly competitive world of European rallying, and (2) he did it on standard BFGoodrich "street tires"—an admitted handicap in a sport dominated by the specialty rally tires of Pirelli, Dunlop, and Michelin.

The use of BFG street tires prompted one English writer to comment: "American tyres? You'll probably mutter, Sheesh, bloody 'orrible great wide things which look like radials but aren't and 'ave nasty white letters sticking out the side and are passable in the dry but terrible in the wet and are only made for Cadillacs or somethin' and don't come in proper 13 inch sizes anyway . . . ."

By placing second on the Tour of Cumbria with his beat-up Triumph and his American street tires, described as "great wide things which look like radials but aren't"—JB generated a lot of media interest . . . .

152

**JB:** "When we first went to Europe with BFGoodrich street tires, the European rally journalists could not believe we were using stock assembly line street tires. They kept asking what kind of special compounds we were using and when I tried to tell them they were the same tires BFG sold to the public, they said we must be having a language problem and they'd ask again, 'What kind of compounds are they using in these special tires?'

In fact when we first put the BFGoodrich decals on the rally car, most people didn't know what they meant and we had to add a separate decal reading 'Tires' (or 'Tyres' for fans in England) because people did not know BFG was a U.S. tire company."

The cover of England's *Rally Sport* magazine featured JB's Triumph on a stage in Germany and announced, "Achtung, Herr Buffum! Captain America's German Adventure." Meanwhile, as Buffum was busily spreading bits and pieces of his TR-8 across Europe and his Audi 4000 across the U.S., and managing the American Peugeot team, Audi Motorsports' new rally program was progressing quite nicely. On the Monte Carlo Rally in January, Hannu Mikkola held a six-minute lead after six snow-covered stages. But just before dawn of the second day, Hannu admitted his foot slipped off the brake pedal, and without warning, he put the Quattro into a bridge abutment, breaking a wheel as well as some engine and suspension bolts. After some very lengthy repairs he was again challenging the leaders when he went off the road "in very frightening circumstances" as the brake pedal went to the floor.

Just hours before his Monte Carlo crash, Mikkola's crew informed him he'd just become a new father.

A few weeks later, Audi's fortunes improved as Mikkola and co-driver, Arne Hertz, won the Swedish Rally, breaking a thirty-one-year-old tradition of repeated victories by Swedish drivers. Audi had already won the Janner Rally in Austria, but the Swedish win was the factory's first world championship victory.

Then a thirty-one year-old French woman, Michele Mouton, shocked the rally world by winning the San Remo Rally in a Quattro. Her victory set a record that could never be broken: Michele was the first woman to ever win a world championship rally! Mikkola then finished the year on a high note, winning the RAC World Championship Rally in England.

It appeared that Audi Motorsports' drive towards a future world championship was right on schedule.

In the U.S., John Buffum commented, during an interview near the end of the '81 season, "I'm hoping to have a Quattro sometime next year, but right now it's anybody's guess. And as far as all the rumors go about seeing a Quattro rally car in this country before the end of the year, I'm 95 percent certain it just won't happen."

# 14

## The Terminator
### Cookbook Quattro

**W**HEN THE 1981 SEASON ended every automotive manufacturer in the world knew as a certainty that the days of two-wheel-drive rally cars had come to an end. A new era had begun.

The planning that would eventually cause the all-wheel-drive revolution, both in passenger and competition vehicles, actually began in 1977.

What is the difference between "four-wheel" and "all-wheel" drive? There is no difference. The terms are interchangeable, except in advertising buzz words. For many years the term "four-wheel-drive" referred to off-road utility vehicles, such as the American Motors Jeeps. When four-wheel-drive was developed for passenger automobiles, advertising hucksters introduced the term "all-wheel-drive" to sell the buying public on the concept. It was as if to say, "We're talking *cars* here, folks, not two-ton, mountain-climbing, mud-slogging, behemoths with knobby tires and blinding roof lights."

Audi NSU came into being in 1909 with the merger of two previously independent companies: Auto Union and NSU. That same year the new company began its rally activities with a light-weight NSU, winning the Prince Henry Rally. In 1913 the Audi name again surfaced when a car designed by August Horch, featuring radical new brake technology, won the Alpine Rally.

Development work on a full time all-wheel-drive system began in earnest in the spring of 1977 when an Audi development engineer named Jorg Benzinger, completed a cross-country test drive of a 4WD VW Iltis and decided 4WD should be made available in passenger cars. The Iltis was actually developed by Audi but because of political reasons it was produced under the VW label. Audi's Iltis beat out bids by Porsche and Daimler-Benz when the West German government was seeking a replacement for the DKW Munga 2-stroke 2WD military vehicle.

Benzinger convinced the mostly skeptical Audi management that all-wheel-drive was the wave of the future when he drove a standard looking Audi 4000 up an impossibly steep grassy hill across from their corporate offices—in the rain! Afterward he revealed that the drive train was actually four-wheel-drive.

By 1978 prototypes A1 to A20 were created, "A" — standing for "Allrad" all wheel drive. The following year, FISA, a division of the FIA international governing body, declared all-wheel-drive legal for world championship rallies and Audi introduced the first "R-Wagen"—the "R" prefix indicating the car was intended for rallying.

The new all-wheel-drive automobile was dubbed "Quattro" by Walter Treser, manager of Audi's development department. He thought of the name after studying an Italian cookbook! The car was introduced to an astounded public in the spring of 1980 at the Geneva Motor Show.

In 1980 Audi formed a special Motor Sport Division in Ingolstadt (Bavaria) to develop the Quattro rally program. They hired Hannu Mikkola, a thirty-nine-year-old Finnish rally driver who had emerged as a star in 1968, driving a Ford Escort TC to first place on the 1000 Lakes Rally. Also in 1980 Freddy Kottulinsky drove a 4WD Iltis to first place in the car class of the prestigious Paris-Dakar Rally.

When the 1982 world rally championship season began it was already obvious the all-wheel-drive Audi Quattro held an astonishing technical advantage over every other car then in existence. In 1982 the Audi Quattro won seven of twelve world championship rallies and in four years it had taken twenty-one world championship wins, equaling, and later breaking Ford's earlier record established with the Escort.

Audi won the World Championship for Manufacturers in 1982 and, nearing the end of the season, Michele Mouton held a slim lead over Walter Rohrl (Opel Ascona 400) in the World Championship for Drivers. But she missed her chance to make history as the first female world rally champion when she rolled her Audi while leading the 4,000 km Ivory Coast Rally.

The 100 mph roll blew out the windshield and co-driver, Fabrizia Pons, lost her pacenotes. Local natives put the car back on its wheels and Michele motored on with Fabrizia using the very confusing and imprecise event route book. Fifteen kilometers further, Pons called a junction straight on with a road coming in from the right, but when the heavy fog cleared, the junction was completely different. Michele had no chance. She went off the road at speed and the resulting damage was terminal to her chances. Walter Rohrl motored by to win the event and the world championship. Michele Mouton finished second—still the highest placing ever held by a female in the male-dominated world of international rallying.

The following year, Audi finished second in the manufacturers standings, but team driver Hannu Mikkola captured the driver's crown. In 1984 Audi again proved its total domination, winning both the manufacturers title and the driver's championship for Stig Blomqvist.

John Buffum got his first Audi Quattro in 1982 . . . .

**JB:** "I missed the first two U.S. championship rallies in 1982 when Audi had us ship our two-wheel drive 4000s back to Europe. Then in February, Jo Hoppen finally said I would get a Quattro and almost before he hung up the telephone I had Salty and John Beauvais on a flight to Germany.

They worked two weeks at the Audi Sport facilities in Ingolstadt (just north of Munich), rebuilding Quattro chassis No. 27. It was the same car Michele Mouton and her Italian co-driver, Fabrizia Pons, had used to win the world championship rally in Portugal the week before. It was the only time the car had been rallied but its hood and top were all caved in from the crew jumping up and down on it—celebrating.

My deal with Audi and Jo Hoppen was always very nebulous. I never had a written contract during my eight years with Audi. Hoppen was just not a paperwork kind of person. He was a modern man of the old world where a simple

*14.1 1982: JB's first Audi Quattro (Chassis #27), the same car Michele Mouton drove to first place in the Portugal world championship rally. Here Michele shows JB the decal from Portugal, still mounted inside the trunk lid. (Photo: Martin Holmes)*

handshake was as binding as any fifty-page document. I think I got that first Quattro, parts, and about $6,000 per rally in 1982. I'm not sure what would have happened if I'd asked for a written contract. Hoppen may have just said, 'You don't trust me?' and canceled the whole deal. But I do trust people and I never mentioned a contract.

The new car had a 131 cubic inch (2144 cc) 320 hp engine, five in-line cylinders, a single KKK turbocharger boosting intake pressure to two and a half atmospheres (1.5 bars), an air-to-air intercooler, fifteen inch alloy wheels, and it weighed 2,535 pounds. It was beautiful!

In April we flew the car 3,000 miles from Germany to New York City then Salty and John Beauvais trailered it 3,000 more miles to the west coast. In fact, the first time I saw the car was the day before the start of the Nor'wester PRO Rally in Washington.

We began winning right from the start, although we were a bit lucky on that first rally. Millen was leading midway through because I was trying to drive the car like a front-wheel-drive car: steering with the brake and losing time in the corners. Then Millen's Mazda overheated and vapor locked and he was passed by several cars. When he got going again he caught Guy Light but Light couldn't see him in all the dust so Millen gently tapped his rear bumper—at speed—until Light moved over.

At the finish control, Millen was parked, waiting for his timing sticker when Light arrived and purposely drove into the rear of his Mazda in retaliation for the earlier bump. The deed cost Guy Light a few hundred dollars for repairs to Millen's car and a reprimand from the SCCA. The problems compounded to cost Millen the rally, otherwise he would have won. **"**

"Began winning right from the start" is certainly an understatement of the facts. The marriage of John Buffum and

159

Audi Quattro was one only a rival could hate. During their first full year in the new Quattro, JB and Doug Shepherd won ten national championship rallies in North America, nine in the U.S. and one in Canada. In fact, there were only two times the Quattro did not win. After eight straight victories, the Quattro suffered its only DNF of the year when JB broke its rear suspension and parked it atop a very large rock on the Tostitos Coronado Rally in Arizona, with disappointed English co-driver, Neil Wilson, on board. Then JB enjoyed a leisurely drive through the Nevada desert on the final rally of the year—The Reno International–and finished second to win the manufacturer's, driver's, and co-driver's championships of the United States.

**JB:** "While we were having great success with the Quattro here in the U.S., the factory works teams were having teething problems we never experienced. Ours ran like a train, very tough, and very dependable—because we used tried and true parts and stuck with them. The factory was constantly tearing down the works cars, trying to improve them, always fiddling with something new, so they were working out a lot of problems and sometimes creating new ones for themselves. It just proves the wisdom in the saying: If it ain't broke, don't fix it."

The Audi Quattro, with John Buffum behind the wheel, was so devastating it prompted one magazine writer to dub it "The Terminator."

**JB:** "The Quattro was the only all-wheel-drive rally car in North America at that time and it was such a superior machine I was afraid SCCA might ban it as the FIA had banned four-wheel-drive some years before. So, on more than one occasion, I stopped in the middle of stages to keep the scores closer.

The first time was in Ohio. The roads were tight and twisty and favored the Audi's all-wheel-drive, acceleration, and power, and we'd built up about a ten minute lead. I stopped in the middle of a stage and told Doug Shepherd to start a watch and let me know when forty-five seconds had passed. I didn't want to kill a full minute and let the next car catch me.

Doug got a bit upset but told me the time and I took off again. At the finish of the rally several journalists asked me why I'd won so many stages so easily—except this one particular stage. What had happened?

'Why nothing, of course!'

Sometimes I'd just slow down on a few stages to keep the scores closer. We did that several times during '82 and '83. **"**

Despite dashing from coast to coast, winning almost every rally he entered, JB found time to run the Pikes Peak Auto Hill Climb and, on July 4th weekend, he set a new record as the fastest production car driver in the sixty year history of that famed event. (Details of Buffum's "race to the clouds" are included in Part Four of this book.) He also found time for another European adventure . . . .

**JB:** **"**At the beginning of 1982 I bought a works prepared Talbot Sunbeam-Lotus. It was the final car produced by the factory to full rally specs and was a front-engine, rear-wheel drive version of Chrysler's Omni-Horizon. With major backing from BFGoodrich, I contracted with Little Brothers of Carlisle, England to maintain and service the car. They had serviced the Talbots in the world championships the prior year. I also hired my old friend, Neil Wilson, as my co-driver.

In February I did the Mintex International in England—a British open championship rally. I put us off the road and we DNFed. We had better luck two months later in Sicily on the

161

Group Two. At the Hunsruck in West Germany the steering broke and dropped us to a tenth place finish.

Then in November I filled our U.S. Quattro with spare parts and had it flown to England for the RAC Rally.**"**

*Autosport* magazine printed JB's comments on his RAC drive:

"It's frustrating because I've put so much effort into doing well in the RAC since I first ran it in 1978. And, what's even more frustrating is the fact the RAC is a 'secret' rally like those in the U.S., which should give me an advantage. Not only that, but the forest roads are similar to those we use in America.

I am especially leery of Kielder, the largest man-made forest in Europe. It is a forbidding place. I can't think of any part of the world in the sport I treat more carefully than Kielder. It is extremely difficult, and very easy to make a mistake. The ground is so soft that if you go off, it's almost impossible to get back on, even if the car is able to continue. Every time I come out of the Kielder, and I know it's over, I'm relieved."

The '82 RAC started in York and promised to be a battle between Opel Ascona 400s and Audi Quattros. Opel's impressive team included Walter Rohrl, who had already wrapped up the '82 world championship for drivers to go along with his 1980 title; Ari Vatanen, 1981 world driving champion; and Henri Toivonen, winner of the 1980 RAC. Audi countered with Hannu Mikkola, winner of the 1981 RAC; Michele Mouton, the remarkable woman who had barely missed the '82 driving championship; Harald Demuth, the German national champion; Malcolm Wilson of British rally fame; and John Buffum, six-time American national champion.

162

The drama did not wait for the opening curtain before beginning in earnest as Opel announced, the night before the start, that they had fired Walter Rohrl for missing a team party and for "lack of interest." The fact that Rohrl had already signed with Lancia for 1983 may have been a contributing, but unstated factor.

Markku Alen, a Finnish driver, surprised everyone by putting his Lancia into an early lead. But it was short-lived as Mikkola pushed past him on Sunday night and drove his Audi Quattro away from the field to win the rally, and the 1982 world championship for manufacturers, four days later.

At the end of the first thirty-six hour loop Buffum was pleased with his start. He'd posted fastest time on two stages, run second on two others, fourth on three, fifth on three, sixth on five, and was sitting fifth overall—against the best professional rally drivers in the world!

In the press interview JB said, "It really was fantastic. I was right, the car was right, and the tires were right. If we accomplished nothing else, I feel we made a point. We were noticed."

By Tuesday, JB's Quattro had sustained considerable body damage but was still running in the top ten positions overall despite the fact two broken half shafts had reduced it to rear-wheel-drive only. Then he began the Kielder stages . . . .

**JB:** "On the first Kielder stage we stopped to change one of the few flats we had on the entire rally. But when it happened the second time, we didn't stop, and in retrospect, that was a mistake. At the time, however, we thought we could make it to the end of the stage.

But finally we came around this very tight right-hander, the car under steered off the outside and dropped six feet below the road level on its side in a ditch. If it hadn't been for the spectators and the fact we were driving a Quattro we'd never have gotten back on the road. As it was, we lost thirteen minutes and any chance we might have had of moving up."

Buffum came out of Kielder in twelfth place and held that position for his first ever finish on the RAC Rally.

It was a very successful year, but it was not without its moments of comedy and tragedy.

The "Ghost of Stuffum Buffum" provided the comedy—a strip of six action pictures, taken by Trackside Photos at a rally press day, appeared in *4-Wheel & Off-Road* magazine. The first two showed Buffum's Quattro powering through a corner, balanced on two wheels, leaning towards the co-driver's side. These two pictures were used on many event posters over the next several years. The following four photos show the Quattro rolling over and landing on its roof —like a turtle!

Buffum's comment: "I hate press days."

Leonard Emanuelson, editor of *Hot Rod* magazine, riding in the co-driver's seat, commented, "I think my watch stopped."

The tragedy occurred in Oklahoma. Tim Cline covered the story for *AutoWeek* magazine:

"Broken Bow, Oklahoma—A fatal accident claimed the lives of two New Zealanders in a sports car rally in the forest just north of this community.

"So began the press bulletin announcing the first deaths ever to occur in U.S. PRO rallying. John Woolf and Grant Whittaker were killed instantly when their Peugeot 504 slammed head-on into a rally workers' 4WD vehicle. The accident happened on Stage Six of the 17-stage Chisum Trail PRO Rally, the sixth round of the 14-event SCCA PRO Rally Championship. The workers, who were not seriously hurt, had apparently stumbled onto the stage

*14.2 1982: JB: "I hate press days." Leonard Emanuelson, editor of* Hot Rod *magazine: "I think my watch stopped." (Photo: Trackside Photo Enterprises)*

in error.

"The Chisum Trail was immediately canceled, and all competition ended.

"Woolf and Whittaker, both twenty-six, died as they had lived, together as inseparable friends doing the thing they loved the most, rallying. They were not great celebrities. Not great sports heroes. Their names were not household words.

"John Woolf—quiet, serious, driver extraordinaire. It was fun to watch him drive. He went with gusto, throwing the car, attacking the course, using every inch of the road and then some.

"Grant Whittaker—outgoing and friendly with eyes that flashed with excitement. "Should be a good rally, eh?"

165

IN LIKE A LAMB . . . OUT LIKE A LION

He said that before every event. Dry or wet, long or short, warm or cold, large entry or small, Grant always knew that it was going to be a good event.

"As the word spread among the crews about the accident, a pall settled over the rally. We wanted to scream, 'No, it's not true. People don't get hurt rallying. There is some kind of mistake. This is the motor sport where the cars get rolled up into little balls and the drivers walk away and we make jokes about it.'

"I just can't shake the feeling that we're still going toget together after the rally. John and I will have a beer, and he will tell about how he almost went into the woods holding both hands out in front of himself like in an airplane, showing how the car tipped but didn't go over.

"Grant will have at least one story about how he outfoxed a control crew, and we'll all sit around the pool and talk about their new car which is nearly finished and which they will be running at the next event.

"We've got lots to talk about."

It was the first time Woolf and Whittaker had drawn the number one starting position since they began rallying in the U.S. two years earlier.

It happened again in November during a massive blizzard at the Press On Regardless PRO Rally in the Upper Peninsula of Michigan. Larry Newland, a seed six driver from Wisconsin, died instantly when his Jeep flew off a snow-covered bridge at the finish line of a special stage and slammed into a tree. His co-driver, Ed White, was severely injured but survived.

Mary Buffum recalls that sobering year:

"I used to worry about John all the time. I didn't care if he lost, I just worried about him getting hurt. I remember a rally in California when he ran out of gas. He was running

166

with Ken Adams and they parked the car and covered it with shrubs and branches so nobody would see it. I heard all sorts of stories. He'd crashed. He was on fire. All kinds of things.

"People are so gory. They love to talk about the accidents. It wasn't fun for me or any of the other women who were waiting for their husbands or boyfriends to pass by in the woods.

"I finally stopped going to rallies because it scared me too much. What finally finished it was when Woolf and Whittaker died on Memorial Day in Oklahoma.

"John called me that day and said, 'I'm okay but there's been a bad accident.'

"For a long while I believe John just thought I was being silly worrying all the time and I know Doug Shepherd was always telling his wife, Toni, that she worried too much. But that accident finally made them see what could happen and why we worried so.

"I've never stopped worrying and I've never gone to a rally again. John and Thumper [Mary's son, Paul Choiniere, Jr.] have an agreement with me. They call as soon as they can after the finish of every rally, or after they finish, whichever comes first.

But I never stop worrying until I get that call."

As the year drew to a close, the American Auto Racing Writers & Broadcasters Association announced the selection of its ten-member 1982 All-American Racing Team. The awards, announced on the "Motorweek Illustrated" broadcast over WTBS-TV in Atlanta, were presented to Rick Mears and Gordon Johncock (OpenWheel), Bobby Allison and Darrell Waltrip (Stock Cars), Al Unser Jr. and John Paul Jr. (Road Racing), Shirley Muldowney and Lee Shepard (Drag Racing), and Michael Andretti and John Buffum (At Large).

1982 marked the first time a rally driver was ever named to the annual All-American Racing Team.

# 15
## Return on Investment
### Flying Mechanics in Africa

**W**HEN JOSEF HOPPEN put John Buffum behind the wheel of an Audi Quattro, he created a monster—a combination that totally dominated the North American professional rally circuits for six years.

Those involved in the sport watched in awe as JB and the Quattro destroyed the competition and marveled at his good luck in acquiring the best ride in the U.S. or Canada. During rallies, other competitors often left their cars and walked to the start line of a stage just to watch the Quattro roar away and disappear into the night. For them, it was both an exhilarating and discouraging sight.

But the reasons for JB's good luck were often overlooked—the years of hard work; the Stuffum Buffum dog days; the months away from home; the hundreds of dreary motel rooms and fast food joints; the thousands of nerve-testing rally miles; the bitter hard-learned lessons; the injuries and the losses.

Luck had nothing to do with it.

JB was like the man who said, "I don't understand it. The harder I work, the more I practice, the luckier I get."

Years ago some pundit said, "Good judgment comes from experience, and experience comes from bad judgment." John

Buffum's years of experience, marred by moments of bad judgment, had come to an end.

Those six years were the payoff on many years of investment.

During that span of years JB drove his Audi at a record-setting pace which may never be equaled. From 1982 through 1987 he entered sixty-six national championship rallies in North America and won fifty-two of them. He took seven seconds, one fourth, and DNFed only five times. One rally in Texas was canceled.

Of his fifty-two victories, fourteen were in Canada, where he posted a 100 percent winning record.

Buffum was the SCCA National PRO Rally driving champion each of those six years; the North American Rally Cup driving champion five of the six years, and Audi took five national championships for manufacturers.

But it didn't end there. In three of his six Quattro years he was elected to the ten member All-American Racing Team by the American Auto Racing Writers & Broadcasters Association, and, in 1987 he received the Robert V. Ridges Memorial Award—the highest honor the Sports Car Club of America can bestow on a rallyist.

Despite all that JB still found time to run many overseas events; to win two One Lap of America Rallies, the Alcan 5000 Rally to Alaska and back, and post two record-setting wins at the Pikes Peak Auto Hill Climb.

When he retired at the end of 1987 it must have seemed those six years passed by far too quickly, like hitting the fast-forward button on a VCR. Still, there were memorable moments . . . .

**JB:** "When the 1983 season began we all had high hopes for the continued growth of professional rallying in North America. The SCCA hired Tom Grimshaw as the PRO Rally

National Series Steward which meant we would have continuity between events. In past years, event stewards were selected by the PRO Rally Board. Each rally had a different steward, usually from the local area, and many of them had no stage rally experience at all. But now we wouldn't have to deal with different stewards, and differing rules interpretations, at every event. It was another step forward for our sport.

When the '82 season ended we heard a lot of rumors concerning a four-wheel-drive Mazda. Mazda didn't have a 4WD model back then, so we weren't sure what was going on.

Then Rod Millen came out with a 4WD Mazda RX-7 that he had developed, with help from Peter Weismann, a west-coast transmission expert. Millen used bits and pieces from the front-wheel-drive 626, shifted the 130B engine back to make room for the steering rack and took the front-end drive direct from the gearbox without using a transfer case.

The car was very good, although not equal to the old Quattro I was running that year.

I won most of the U.S. rallies in '83, but in Washington I finished second behind Millen when I caught a stump on a stage and put the Quattro on its roof. But I got even.

That year there were two Washington rallies a week apart, the Olympus and Nor'wester. The organizers called it 'Rally Week Northwest' and generated a lot of national media attention.

We all stayed at the Tyee Motor Inn between the events and it was a week-long party.

After his win at the Olympus, Millen went home to California. But he left a hundred dollars of his contingency prize money behind and we spent most of it buying drinks all around in the Tyee bar. When he came back a week later for the second rally we had his change—I think it was about eight dollars and some coins—mounted in a glass-covered frame together with a paper we all signed, thanking him.

171

Rod and I were both running for BFGoodrich that year and we presented his 'change trophy' to him during a dinner with several BFG reps. Being a tight Kiwi, he wasn't very happy, but the setting left him no choice but to grit his teeth, smile and go along with the joke. Paybacks are a bitch.

Then I made things worse by beating him the next weekend.**"**

*15.1 1983 Olympus PRO Rally: JB (white uniform) surveys the results of "catching a stump" while guest co-driver, Steve Fellows, of* Motoring News, *prepares to hitchhike home. (Photo: Su Kemper)*

In May 1983, professional rallying in North America received the stamp of legitimacy from *Sports Illustrated*. Sam Moses wrote a full-length feature on his experiences as JB's co-driver during his winning run on the '82 Tour de Forest PRO Rally in Washington. The following excerpts capture the sensations of an amateur first-time co-driver riding through the mountains with one of the fastest drivers in the world:

"There are strange things going on in the woods at night, stirring things, thrilling things, dangerous things, things that we don't hear much about and that if we ever came upon by chance might affect us like a close encounter of another kind.

"Imagine yourself camping in a forest at 3:00 A.M., and you're awakened by a muted howl, far in the distance. It grows closer, far too rapidly to be alive. It sounds mechanical, or unearthly if your imagination tends toward that sort of interpretation. The pitch of the howl rises and falls and the thing approaches as a glow through the trees, and it passes through your mind that in seconds the world is going to end. Finally, the thing bursts upon you with an explosion of brilliant lights and a roaring engine, and you say, 'Is that a car?' but you can't believe it because cars don't move sideways. Then you catch a glimpse of two men inside, apparently controlling it, and after it passes the big yellow lights become smaller red ones, taillights that tell you for sure it's a car. The taillights chase the headlights off into the woods at about 70 mph, and the howl tapers away. You look back in the direction it came from. There's another one coming

". . . A rally driver needs superb car control and a lion's heart. 'Trying to read the roads going that fast at night is like trying to read in a foreign language,' says Buffum. 'You don't have time to translate it, you've got to think in that language. When trees come out of the dark ahead of me, I can't be thinking about what that means. I have to be able to sense them if I'm going to react quickly enough.'

". . . The turbo whines as it is unbound. Stones smash against the skid plate under the chassis as all four wheels

173

churn. At this point the car is usually still so far sideways that Buffum's arms are completely crossed on the steering wheel; they untwist back to nine o'clock and three o'clock, and he speeds off toward the next turn, the turbo's whine building like the sound of a spaceship taking off in a science-fiction movie. Buffum upshifts at 7,000 rpm without watching the tachometer, so intent is he with the task at hand outside the windshield. Nothing distracts him, not even the trees whizzing past the Quattro's windows, branches clicking against the door handles as it speeds down the pencil-thin logging road in the dead of night.

". . . Buffum occasionally mumbles to himself, and through the headset he sounds like Ray Charles groaning to his music at the piano. Buffum's feet play passionately on his own pedals, creating the rhythmic whine and chirp of the turbo, and even the shattering of stones on the skid plate seems part of some outrageous original melody.

". . . There was a stage in the rally called Bingham Creek; it was the longest at 20.78 miles. It was also Buffum's favorite, breathtaking, winding around the walls of a deep canyon, the gravel road everywhere 'exposed,' as the route book noted. That's the same ominous message one finds in rock climbing guide books, and it means: If you fall there, you're going straight down for a while.

"The hairpin turns on the stage were on the face of the canyon walls, and the broad beams of the six high-intensity headlights sprayed light into the black void beyond the edge. Buffum threw the Quattro into the turns, one foot hard on the throttle and the other bouncing on the brake, the turbo howling and the stones thrown God only knows how far.

". . . Buffum won the first two rallies of 1983 as easily as he had won most of them last year. In the third rally, Buffum introduced his new Quattro, which has the same

174

features as the last one, and Millen unveiled his new car: a 4WD Mazda RX-7 that he had built himself. It was a giant-killing effort: a small shop in California vs. an entire factory in Germany. Buffum won again. But in only its second rally, on April 17, the Mazda upset the Quattro. Buffum literally upset himself, rolling the Quattro on its roof during the event, a fairly common and usually harmless occurrence for a rally driver, but still humbling for Buffum. But the message had been sent, the gauntlet thrown. Buffum and the Quattro would not have it all their way with the series this year, as they had in 1982."

**JB:** "Late in the year (1983) we ran a snow rally, The Sno-Drift, in Michigan. My car was still in England for the RAC so I borrowed my old Quattro from Bruno Kreibich. He'd bought it from Audi at the end of the previous year.

On the Avery Lake Stage we slid off the road into a bank and lost all forward gears. So we had to drive to the end of the stage (2½ miles) in reverse. We were then towed 20 miles to the next service area. When we got close to service I ran over a whole line of mailboxes on wooden posts and Shepherd had to take time to set them all back up while I was still trying to reach our crew.

We couldn't continue with the broken gearbox and DNFed. Bruno was at the rally, watching. He wasn't real happy.

In October I went to Africa to drive a Quattro chase car in the Ivory Coast World Championship Rally. The rally started and ended in Abidjan. It was a non-stage rally where the teams ran flat out for 4500 kilometers over five days.

The trick to winning was to keep the car running and Audi and Toyota came up with the idea of 'flying mechanics'—a fully-prepared rally car, with a mechanic on board (I had two in my car), chasing the competition cars at full speed throughout the rally. It meant I had to drive nearly as fast, and sometimes even faster, than Mikkola's Quattro. He was the only driver entered by Audi.

The world championship rules required a minimum entry of fifty cars back then and the Ivory Coast was short a few entrants so both Toyota and Audi entered their chase cars to get them up to the limit. Then we dropped back and ran as support cars for five days.

Back in 1979, the first year of the world driver's championships, Hannu Mikkola won the Ivory Coast Rally. Bjorn Waldegard finished second and went on that year to become the first official world driving champion. In 1983, Waldegard won The Ivory Coast in a Toyota Celica Twin cam Turbo and Mikkola came second with his Audi Quattro—but, Mikkola went on that year to win the world driving championship. It was an exact reversal of 1979.

When I came home from Africa I was sicker than a dog. I either had some bug or a bad case of heat stroke from playing golf in temperatures over 100°.

I wasn't in any shape to drive the next U.S. rally which was the POR in Michigan so Audi brought Hannu in to run in my place. It was very good for our sport to have the world champion running in the U.S. national championship series.

Fabrizia Pons, Michele Mouton's co-driver, also came over to ride with Hannu and, of course, they won the POR and kept Millen and Mazda from taking first place points.

In '83 FISA President, Jean-Marie Balestre, expressed interest in having a world championship rally in the United States. There were three U.S. events trying for a WRC spot: The Olympus in Washington, The Carson City International in Nevada, and The Michigan International. Unfortunately FISA sent Jean Paul Todt to observe the Michigan event.

It was an absolute disaster. The organizer's ideas were very good: start in downtown Detroit at the Renaissance Center to capture media attention; run a spectator stage in

*15.2 1983: Ivory Coast World Championship Rally, Africa. JB and the two "flying mechanics," Franz and Holdi, stuffed inside the Audi Quattro chase car jammed full of spare parts to support Hannu Mikkola's second place finish. (Photo: Martin Holmes)*

*15.3 1983: Ivory Coast Rally—JB making use of an African tow truck following a slight off-course excursion.*

177

Detroit on the Michigan State Fairgrounds; then move up north to Cadillac for two more days of real rallying in the woods.

The organization and execution were horrible.

At the end of the opening stage on the fairgrounds we had to run up a ramp into the second floor of a building where pigs were displayed during the state fair, then down a ramp to a finish line. The instructions were so nebulous and the course so poorly marked that we were the only car of the first three who ran through the Pig Building. Millen and Woodner went around it, in different directions.

I was so mad I jumped out of the car at the finish and bounced my helmet about ten feet off the roof of the Quattro.

Fortunately, the SCCA steward was there and canceled the stage before someone ran over a spectator or into another car.

It was all downhill from there. One hour waits at the start of stages up north. Forest authorities holding up the rally while they drove every inch of every road. Stages canceled because of lack of start/finish communications. A real fiasco.

I won with Neil Wilson as my co-driver, but I was really upset with the image we portrayed for the FISA observer.

Still, there were some good things. When we paraded the rally cars through downtown Cadillac, every store window had a painting of a different team. The town had organized a competition among the local school kids. That was quite good.

The Michigan International PRO Rally only ran that one time.

During 1983 my co-driver, Doug Shepherd, let me know he intended to move into the driver's seat the following year. He'd been running his own Dodge Colt on lower level divisional rallies and was doing very well.

When I received my national championship award at the year-end banquet in Carson City I thanked Doug for the many years we'd had together; six very successful and very enjoyable years; and I wished him good luck with his new career as a driver. I was already thinking about who I would team with in 1984. As it turned out, I used several people.**"**

*15.4 1983 Lombard RAC Rally (England): Service crew makes hurried repairs to JB's Quattro while Neil Wilson checks the time.*

*15.5 JB and Neil Wilson arriving at the finish of the 1983 Lombard RAC World Championship Rally (England).*

# 16
## A B-i-i-i-g Moment
### Close Call In Pennsylvania

*E* ARLY IN 1984, the major manufacturing companies interested in supporting the SCCA's professional rally series met to demand some changes in the overall management of the national program. They backed their demands with substantial financing and the SCCA immediately accepted their suggestions.

First, they elevated Tom Grimshaw from the position of National Steward to National PRO Rally Manager, responsible for all aspects of the championship series; safety, scheduling, event organization, sanctioning, and conduct of all competition at the national level. The five member SCCA PRO Rally board, which had managed the overall conduct of the national series since its inception in 1973, was placed in charge of the newly introduced "divisional" series of lower level training events. The board was chaired by Virginia Reese, a Michigan co-driver who had run with the Fiat factory team some years earlier and was currently co-driving for Jon Woodner.

The most surprising move—certainly the most exciting to everyone involved in the sport—was the announcement that the SCCA had hired Jim Porter, the organizational genius who had built England's RAC Rally into one of the most prestigious international championship events in the world. Porter was to move his family to the U.S. near the end of the year.

Securing Jim Porter was a real coup for the SCCA. He was recognized as one of the best, if not the very best, rally organizers in the entire world. He was a man who was used to dealing with the multi-million dollar world of international rallying. He was a respected professional; the absolute perfect choice to move the United States of America into the center ring of the international rally circus.

But . . . as the time neared for Jim Porter's appearance in the U.S., the SCCA panicked, and their National PRO Rally Championship Series suffered a blow that relegated it to the backburner——where it remains today.

Porter was to make his first appearance at the final rally of the season—The Carson City (Nevada) International. Everyone eagerly awaited his arrival, including representatives from every company involved in the PRO Rally Series.

Then SCCA dropped its bombshell. They issued a press release announcing that Porter would **not** be coming to the U.S. and would **not** be hired by the SCCA.

While everyone in Carson City was reading this unbelievable message, Martin Holmes, England's world renown rally reporter and photographer, rushed to the telephone and contacted Jim Porter at his home in England. Martin's call was the first time Porter learned that his deal with the SCCA had been canceled.

It was a shabby way to treat anyone, much less a man of Jim Porter's world wide stature. It also sent a message to everyone involved in the sport—the SCCA did not intend for its own national championship professional rally series to be much more than a low level club activity.

The supporting manufacturers got the message and put their checkbooks back into their pockets. BFGoodrich Tire Company packed its bags and moved on. Their loss was the most serious blow of all. It was the beginning of a long slide for pro rallying in North America. Suddenly it was like someone once said, "The future isn't what it used to be."

Despite all the bad news, some good things happened in '84. FISA sent Jacques Regis from France to observe The Olympus Rally for possible world championship status and his report resulted in the WRC series returning to the U.S. in 1985—after an eleven-year absence.

**JB:** "1984 was the year BFGoodrich sent me to Europe. It was their final big commitment to rallying in our country. It was also the year I used several co-drivers in the U.S., looking for the one who would replace Doug Shepherd.

Harry Ward did a couple of rallies and we won the Nor'wester together in Washington. I won in Michigan with Fred Gallagher and in Pennsylvania with Neil Wilson. My stepson, Paul Choiniere, Jr., co-drove when we won the Lobster Rally in Canada.

Finally I tried Tom Grimshaw for two events, the Dyfi Ste. Agathe in Quebec and the Oregon Trail in Oregon. We won them both and I asked him to run full time in '85.

It was a good choice for both of us. At that point in our careers we'd both been around the block several times. We were thought of as the 'old guard' in the sport. There wasn't much we hadn't seen or done over the years.

And we were both secure enough with our experience and abilities that we were ready to relax and have some fun—while still trying to win every rally we ran, of course.

We had three very good years together—and a lot of fun.

1984 was the year of the 'Great Atomic Food Fight' in Houghton, Michigan.

Neil Wilson came over from England to co-drive the POR for me and we hit a tree the first night and wrecked the Quattro.

183

So we did what everyone does at the POR when they're not driving in the rally, we went to The Library Bar.

The Library Bar was the mecca of professional rallying back then. It was owned by Jon Davis, a very good rally driver who ran Saabs in the early days and won the national production class championship for Saab in 1980 and 1981.

A lot of teams were out of the rally by the second night and they were all at The Library. Grimshaw, John Crawford and I had all crashed in separate cars and sat together at one table. Several Kiwi team members were at another.

Early in the evening I threw a slice of orange at my mechanic, Salty Sottolano. It stuck to his face. He retaliated. The Kiwis joined in by dumping a full pitcher of beer on our table. Before long the air was filled with flying food of every description.

Neil, being a very reserved Englishman, was so embarrassed he moved to a neutral table. Grimshaw left for a time and returned with three umbrellas that he and I and John Crawford used to protect ourselves. They were our 'nuclear umbrellas.'

At one point, we arranged 'SALT' talks with the Kiwis and a truce was declared—until we dumped several salt shakers on them.

The bar employees called the Davis home and pleaded for help. Jon's wife, Marcia, came to the bar, walked in, took one long look, and left.

Someone took a color photo of the three of us sitting under our open umbrellas, which were covered with all sorts of garbage, and it later appeared in a magazine.

When we returned to The Library Bar the following year, Davis had placed a commemorative plaque on the wall over our table—the scene of 'The Great Atomic Food Fight of '84.'

Being a professional rally driver is a very intense and serious occupation.

*A B-i-i-i-g Moment*

Hannu Mikkola returned to the U.S. to drive a Quattro on the final 1984 championship event in Carson city. Doug Shepherd, who had already won the production class driving championship in a Dodge Shelby Charger, co-drove for Hannu.

It was a very good finish for Audi as Quattros finished in the top three positions. Hannu won, we were second and Bruno Kreibich was third. The second place finish gave me the national championship.

Another highlight that year was the golf tournaments that

16.1 *Audi Quattros finish 1-2-3 at the 1984 Carson City International Pro Rally (Nevada) First: Hannu Mikkola (L-atop car) and Doug Shepherd (2nd from left). Second: John Buffum (R-atop car) and Neil Wilson (2nd from right). Third: Bruno Kreibish (far right) and Clark Bond (far left).*

were held at some national rallies. Tom Grimshaw and I paired up to win the first one in Olympia, Washington. Then we lost all the rest of them during the year. It was entirely Grimshaw's

185

fault, although he denies it.

The rift between Rod Millen and me came to an end in 1984 at the Oregon Trail PRO Rally late in the year. I'd won the rally Saturday night but the organizers made us get up early Sunday morning to do some spectator stages on the track at the Portland International Speedway. We were scheduled to do four laps on the track (one car at a time), and a short parking lot solo event around some pylons.

Of course none of us were very happy about all that. Millen and I had had a really close all night battle on slippery mountain roads covered with icy rain and snow, and we didn't look forward to putting on our wet uniforms and doing some silly spectator thing early the next morning. Besides, the Sunday morning bits were not even counted in the final results. The rally was over Saturday night.

So I decided to just motor slowly around the track and through the solo course. Tom and I didn't even hook up our full safety harnesses at the start line.

But then, as a local SCCA race worker was lining us up on the track, Jon Woodner pulled alongside and suggested we start together and have a go at it. Then Rod Millen also pulled up, followed by his brother Steve. That was a bit more interesting. We hooked up our harnesses and our helmets.

The SCCA worker, seeing that four cars were about to go 'racing' at the same time, flipped out. He started screaming for us to shut our engines off and ran around waving his arms in panic. So we relaxed and started to unhook again. Then Woodner took off, followed by Roddy. Steve and I joined in.

The four of us put on a hell of a show racing flat out for several laps, going wheel to wheel, crowding each other in the corners, driving in the grass, laughing like kids.

Each time we passed the start/finish line the SCCA guy waved a black flag at us and jumped around a lot. We ignored him. The crowd was cheering and we were having a hell of a time.

When we finally stopped, Roddy and I got together and traded team jackets and cars for the solo event. Someone took a group photo of us all together, with me wearing a Mazda jacket and Roddy wearing my Audi jacket. Needless to say, that photo never saw the light of day.

I burned most of the rubber off the Mazda's tires and crushed some pylons while Roddy was wrestling in the infield with the Quattro. When he and Grimshaw went off the road for the second or third time Roddy said, 'How the hell does JB drive this rat. It handles like a truck.'

Some weeks later we heard that the SCCA worker tried to get the national office to pull all our rally licenses for ignoring his black flag. I don't think he knew that all four of us also had racing licenses and had spent a lot of time on tracks over the years. Anyway, nothing came of his bitching—except that we had a great time and Rod Millen and I were more relaxed with each other after that day.

1985 was a tough year, both for the sport of professional rallying in the U.S. and for our Audi team.

SCCA continued their PRO Rally Manager program, hiring Bob Radford, a TSD road rallyist who made no secret of the fact that he did not particularly like PRO rallying, but there was a lot of unrest after the Porter fiasco. I think we all knew the best years for professional rallying in our country had come to an end. Some event organizers even got together and invited USAC (United States Auto Club) to take the sport away from SCCA, but nothing came of it.

And the various media forms were beginning to lose interest in us because we had promised the sky for several years and had not delivered. A few years before, when we all—SCCA

187

competitors, manufacturers, organizers, everybody involved in the national series—pulled together to promote PRO rallying as a major U.S. sport, we had some big plans and made some big promises of growth and increased interest. But we were like the boy who cried wolf too many times. Even though we all tried very hard, we didn't deliver on our promises and we finally ran out of time.

Bridgestone Tires sponsored the SCCA PRO Rally Series in 1985. We heard they purchased the entire rights from SCCA for $50,000, but they put their money in the wrong place. They began to pay year-end bonuses of $5,000 to the various class champions. It was a nice gesture but did little to help promote the sport. First, the money wasn't all that much—not enough to attract new blood; and second, the bonuses all went to sponsored teams who were going to run the series anyway— bonus or no bonus.

So, beginning in '85 we all began to change our expectations. We knew we had a tremendously interesting and exciting sport, but we were also beginning to realize it would never be a major public attraction in our country, and the media, realizing the same truth and noting that we were offering nothing new year after year, began to reduce their coverage.

We started the '85 season with a fourth place finish on the opening event—the Nor'wester in Washington. We had fuel problems and couldn't get the Quattro up to speed. Then we broke a rear brake caliper and had a small fire, followed by a front flat and a jack that would not lower so I had to knock it off as we drove away. Later we had to change a broken rear wheel and couldn't get the lug nuts off the bent studs so I had to drive down the highway and snap them off. We ran the rest of the night with only three lug nuts on the rear wheel.

I figured the season was already over for us and I said to Grimshaw, 'Well, at least you can still win the co-driver's championship.'

188

Then, following a win on the Wild West Rally we built a new Group B A2 Quattro for the Susquehannock Trail PRO Rally in Pennsylvania. It didn't last one event.

Around midnight we held about a minute lead on Millen's 4WD Mazda RX-7. Jon Woodner had already hit a tree in another RX-7 and was taken to the hospital with minor injuries.

We were using some notes we had from previous Susquehannock rallies. Although Grimshaw wasn't really familiar with using them and occasionally lost his place, we were going along okay.

Then we made a mistake; he called, 'Flat over crest' as I approached a hill in fifth gear. The road jogged hard right. It was the longest roll either of us had ever experienced and it totally destroyed the new car. Millen later said that when he came along behind us it looked like a 747 had crash-landed in the woods.

I got out and pulled Grimshaw out and laid him on the ground. He kept fading in and out of consciousness while we were waiting for the ambulance. Luckily there was an emergency medical crew at that location and a doctor worked on him while we were waiting. Before the ambulance arrived I noticed Tom's door stuck so high up in a tree that we couldn't reach it. Some corner workers had to shake the tree to get it down. When the ambulance finally arrived and we started out of the woods, the driver got lost and I had to navigate us back to town to reach the hospital.

I called Tom's wife in Kansas City while they were working on him and told her about the accident. She was pretty upset but it all turned out okay. He didn't have any major bones broken like we first thought, just a series of little injuries—a broken right hand (luckily he's left-handed), some cracked ribs, a punctured kidney, and one closed eye.

But he went back to Kansas the following morning and was back in a rally car two weeks later.

*16.2 1985: A $125,000 pile of junk after a b-i-i-i-g moment in Pennsylvania.*

*16.3 1985: JB/Grimshaw/Audi Quattro just before the "fat lady sings" at the end of the Battle Creek PRO Rally (Michigan).*

A month later, in Battle Creek, Michigan, Millen lost a chance to put us away for good that year. The course was exceptionally rough and we'd been braking half-shafts all night so when the morning came he held a half minute lead on us—with one short spectator stage on an army base, before the finish.

Then we got lucky.

He started the final stage in front of us. It was a little two-track trail through the woods—very rough, with big mudholes. Then we came out onto a main gravel road for a short run and almost immediately turned back into the woods onto another little trail. The two turns were included in a single tulip drawing.

I almost missed the second turn back into the woods because I saw Millen's tracks continuing straight down the gravel road. He hadn't turned back into the undergrowth where Grimshaw was yelling for me to turn. After we made the correct turn, I tried to tell Tom that Millen was lost but he couldn't hear me through his intercom, so we ran to the finish before he could understand me. He didn't believe it and made me drive all over the finish area looking for Millen's RX-7.

I don't think he believed it until he saw Millen's car cross the finish line more than a minute behind us. That was the first time I heard the expression, 'It ain't over 'til the fat lady sings.' Sometimes it's better to be lucky than good, or maybe it's best to be good and lucky.

The win in Battle Creek kept us in the hunt and we won the next event in Ohio in a new 420 hp Group B Sport Quattro but rolled on the opening stage of the POR, blew both rear tires, lost the windshield, and cracked the turbo housing. To make matters worse, the organizers got word that a white Audi had forced a lady off the road on a transit and arbitrarily decided it was us and stuck a two minute penalty on our score. Without that two minutes we were leading at the end of the first night. With it, we were second behind Millen.

191

We knew we'd had no encounter with any civilian car so Grimshaw submitted our written protest but the matter was not to be decided until the end of the rally the following day.

For the previous three years, Millen and Mazda had not won any national championships so at the first service halt on the second day of the POR, I took Roddy aside and quietly made a deal that would allow us both to win in '85 . . . I would slow down and let him win the POR, and the manufacturer's championship, if he would slow down on the final rally in Carson City and guarantee us the driving and co-driving championships.

Millen agreed and went on to win the final day. Then true to his word, he did not push us in Carson City and we won the individual championships.

And that is why the SCCA record book shows Tom and I winning the individual championships in 1985 while Mazda won the manufacturer's championship.

To guarantee Millen's win at the POR we withdrew our protest before it could be acted upon. Later we learned that the white Audi in question was a non-rally car being driven around the course by an SCCA official.

1985 was the first year Grimshaw and I ran together—and it was our toughest by far.

The Olympus Rally ran as a prototype world championship event in '85. It was a full pacenote event, just like all other world championship rallies except the RAC in England. Tom and I went to Washington two weeks early to do our notes. Then we bound them into books and sold them to other teams for a couple of hundred bucks. We'd leave early in the morning and do our notes all day long. On the other hand, Hannu Mikkola, the seasoned veteran of European style rallying, would quickly make his notes in the morning and then play golf in the afternoon. However, one afternoon we met Hannu and

192

David and Jill Sutton, who came over from England to observe the rally. David and Jill followed us around in a golf cart and we had a good lunch and good conversation about the state of rallying in North America.

The Olympus was very well done and FISA gave it full world championship status for the next two years. Neil Wilson came over to read notes for me and Grimshaw moved over to run a Dodge Colt with Doug Shepherd. Hannu won the rally. We finished second and Shepherd won the production class.

And we made enough money off the sales of our notes to cover our bar bills.

Our second year together (1986) was not nearly so tough. I signed with Michelin that year and we won the first five events, although we had a close call in Pennsylvania. We were in our motel room watching the women's finals of the French Open Tennis Tournament and lost track of the time before a restart. We then had to run through the town to get to the start on time, and, of course, it was delayed thirty minutes by the organizers. It was a close call. We spent the rest of the rally asking everyone if they knew who won the finals between Chris Evert and Martina Navratilova. Evert won.

In Arkansas the temperature was well over 100° and the organizers brought in a speaker to warn us about heatstroke and what it could do to us. Early on I got into a tight righthander a bit too quickly and went straight off into the woods, but kept my foot in it, knocked down a lot of small trees and popped back out onto the road.

The trees we mowed down did a lot of damage to the front of the car and we had to jump out at the next start line to tear away all the loose pieces. Not long after that I started feeling dizzy and I had to lay down during the following service stop to keep from passing out.

Finally a late afternoon storm bombarded us with large hailstones and a flood of rain, but at least it lowered the

193

temperature. We had two Audi factory mechanics in from Germany to help us in Arkansas. When the storm hit and the trees started bending over to the ground they continued to work on the car. We finally coaxed them into the service van, convincing them—the consummate professionals—that the restart would be delayed. I think a tornado hit pretty close to us but we didn't see it.

The Toyota Olympus World Championship Rally ran in December in Washington. The U.S. rally season was already over and we'd had a fairly easy time winning the national championships.

We were all pretty excited about the Olympus. It was our first world championship rally since the ill-fated POR back in 1974. To add to the excitement, Markku Alen with Lancia and Juha Kankkunen with Peugeot were virtually tied for the world driving title. Because of a still undecided protest against Peugeot on the San Remo Rally, Markku held a one point lead over Kankkunen.

And, on top of everything else going on, the Olympus was to be the final world championship rally for the Group B super cars. Because of several competitor and spectator deaths caused by the 'Killer Bees,' as they were called, FISA had banned Group B beginning the next month, January, 1987.

Grimshaw and I went out early and did the notes again like the year before and Neil Wilson came back to run with me in the Quattro. Tom rode with my stepson, Paul, Jr., in a Group N 4000 Audi.

The previous year Neil had co-driven for Henri Toivonen in a Lancia Delta S4 when they beat Markku Alen to win the RAC World Championship Rally. It was Toivonen's second RAC victory. He'd won it in 1980 in a Talbot Sunbeam Lotus to become the youngest driver (twenty-four years old) to ever win the world's most prestigious professional rally.

194

The Olympus was far and away the most important rally we'd ever held in the U.S. and the organizers, John and Claudia Nagel, and their 1,500 volunteer workers did a hell of a job. It was an excellent rally. It started in the Tacoma Dome on Wednesday night and finished with awards in the marble foyer of the Washington State Capitol Building five days later.

The only sour note was when the guy who plays MacGyver on TV (one of my favorite shows), got in a bit over his head driving the Toyota course-opening car and rolled it into a little ball. Then a worker panicked and drove the wrong way to reach the wreck and met Alen on a stage at speed. Markku was pretty upset but not nearly as mad as the Nagels.

Except for that one incident, the rally went perfectly.

Kankkunen, in a Peugeot 205 T16, and Alen in a Lancia Delta S4, started one, two on the road. I was third and the two Team Toyotas followed me, driven by Waldegaard and Thorp.

Kankkunen took the early lead but gave it up when his service crew cost him a one minute late penalty at a start control while they were replacing the co-driver's computer.

Then Alen got the bit in his teeth and started flying. At the finish he stood on the victory ramp and declared to the crowd, 'I am the world champion.' Two weeks later, FISA denied the San Remo protest and Kankkunen was declared the world driving champion for 1986. Markku had a very short reign.

I was very satisfied with my third place finish in a very tired Quattro. There was no way I was going to touch the Lancia or the Peugeot, unless they had a problem, and we beat the very powerful Toyotas. It was a very good run for me because it was my highest placing on a world championship event and moved me up to Priority A status—the top seed in the FISA world rankings

My stepson also had a great run. In his very first world championship rally, with no prior pace note experience, he

195

finished tenth overall in a Group N stock Audi and won his class by about a day and a half.

I think it may have been that rally, and that very good drive, that finally convinced Paul he had the makings of a first class rally driver.

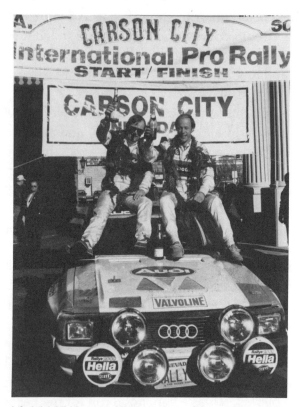

*16.4 1985 National Champions, JB and Grimshaw drink to their victory on the 1985 Carson City International PRO Rally—a happy ending to a very tough year. (Trackside Photo Ent.)*

196

In 1986 Salty Sottolano left me to form his own team for Volkswagen of America. Salty and I had been good friends since we'd met in Germany during our army days. He'd serviced for me on the '69 Monte Carlo Rallye and had run my Libra service crews since 1975. We'd had some great times together over the years but I understood his desire to be on his own and I wished him the best of luck.

John Beauvais, who had joined us in 1981, replaced Salty as Libra's crew chief in 1987. He proved to be a very able replacement and remains in that position today.

At the end of the '86 rally season I thought my years with Audi were over. They were heavily involved in a new racing program and there really wasn't anything left for them to do in rallying in North America. Nothing left to win.

I went home from the Olympus thinking we were all done. I was wrong. In many ways the best was yet to come."

*17.1 World champion, Walter Rohrl, flies a Group B Audi Quattro over a jump.*

# 17
## "B" For Bullet
### The Super Cars

*1* 987 WAS THE END of one chapter in international rallying and the beginning of another. The Group B super cars
were banned and Group A became the flagships of the world
championships.

With a few notable exceptions, the hot rally cars at the end
of the seventies were front-engine, rear-wheel-drive sedans
based loosely on manufacturers' production models. They
weighed a bit more than a ton and carried about 250 hp, which
was all a two-wheel drive car could use. Too much power just
resulted in spinning wheels. The key to speed at that time was
better tires, stronger brakes, manageable suspension and tough,
durable cars. However, extra horsepower did make for great
looking slides through the corners. Traction—getting the power
to the road surface—was the great equalizer in those days.
Then FISA legalized all-wheel-drive in 1979 and changed the
rules of the game.

Suddenly almost unlimited power could be transferred to
the road. It was the beginning of a new era that culminated in
the Group B super cars.

Legalization of rally cars is controlled by rules of
"homologation." Homologation simply means a grouping of
similar parts—in other words, building many copies of the
same car within an established set of specifications.

Homologation rules demand that a predetermined number of copies must be built before the model is accepted for international competition.

In the seventies the dominant homologation group was Group Four which required 1,000 copies of the same vehicle— thus the emphasis on mass produced models for rally use.

In 1983 Groups Two and Four gave way to Group B when FISA introduced very liberal prototype regulations. Group B rules allowed purpose-built rally cars using ultra-light-weight, carbon-fibre body works, plastic windows and space age suspensions—and Group B only required two-hundred copies for homologation!

Several factors came together at the same time, creating what later became known as the "Killer Bees." First, the new all-wheel-drive era removed the previous restrictions on power transference allowing the use of almost unlimited power plants. Secondly, all-wheel-drive proved much easier on tires than two-wheel-drive, so it became possible to introduce much softer compound rally tires offering vastly improved traction. Third, vehicle weight restrictions were virtually non-existent. And finally, the two hundred copies required for legalization created a "run what you brung" theory of rallying taken to unbelievable heights by the unlimited financial and technical resources of automotive manufacturers throughout the world.

The result? A 600 hp, 2,000-pound, all-wheel-drive, screaming banshee. A buzz-bomb bullet such as Lancia's Delta S-4 which accelerated from a dead stop to 60 mph, on a gravel road, in 2.3 seconds! A 500+ hp Audi Sport Quattro so tightly sprung (because of its very short wheel base) that it actually caused a driver's eyeballs to bounce so it often blurred his vision. A car so powerful it cut the decision and reaction time between corners by more than a half. A Lancia Delta rally car that Henri Toivonen drove so fast around a grand prix race course in Portugal that it would have placed sixth on the starting grid of a Formula One race! A Peugeot 205T16 rally car that Nigel Mansell claimed, after a test drive, could out accelerate his Formula One grand prix car. And finally, rally cars that were so fast wings were added to most models in 1985 to create down force.

In short, the Group B rally cars were born killers.

Audi, Peugeot, Lancia, Ford, Citroen and Austin Rover introduced new Group B models that were so powerful many felt they had outstripped a driver's ability to control them. It took three years to prove all the dire predictions were frighteningly correct.

In 1985 Ari Vatanen, the 1981 World Rally Champion, came very close to death when his Group B Peugeot 205T16 crashed during the world championship rally of Argentina.

Between practice and the start of the rally, it rained for several days, creating deep furrows across several stage roads. Vatanen hit one of those new dips at a very high speed, the Peugeot landed on its nose and flipped end-over-end. The crash was so violent, Vatanen's seat broke and he sustained several life-threatening injuries as he bounced around inside the car.

He was flown by helicopter to a hospital in Cordoba where doctors worked feverishly to save his life, and some days later he was flown to a rehab hospital in Helsinki. Miraculously, his co-driver, Terry Harryman, survived the crash with minor injuries. But it would be more than a year, and several operations, before Ari Vatanen was able to return to rallying.

Group B super car technology advanced so quickly it outstripped the ability of FISA to regulate the cars and the ability of organizers to control spectators. The inevitable finally happened on the Port Wine Rally of Portugal. While driving between walls of spectators on the opening stage in the Sintra area, a Ford RS200 left the road, killing three spectators and injuring many others.

Later that same year, Marc Surer nearly died in Germany when his Group B Ford slid off a paved stage, snapped one tree like a toothpick and burst into flame when it slammed into another. The co-driver died in the flames and the accident ended Surer's Formula One career.

In 1986 Michelin rally boss, Maurice Guaslard, fairly summarized the state of professional rallying: "Rallying has reached a point such that the speed limitation is the profile of the road. If everything goes right for the drivers, there is no more than two or three seconds of difference on a stage. Which means the judge is not the cars, the tires, or the drivers—it is the road. They cannot go any faster!"

Where would it stop? It seemed for a time that it not only would not stop, it would soon be even more dangerous. Despite the mounting accident and death rate of Group B, FISA announced they would introduce Group S for futuristic proto-type rally cars that would be even more powerful than Group B—and only ten copies would be required for legal homologation.

The end finally came on May 4, 1986 . . . .

*Autosport* magazine: "Mystery surrounded the death of twenty-nine-year old Henri Toivonen and Sergio Cresto on the 1986 Tour de Corse Rally. No one saw the Lancia Delta S4 plunge from the hillside into trees and, such was the intensity of the subsequent fire, there were no clues from the charred remains of the car's space frame.

The date, May 4, was already etched in the memory of rally fans, for exactly one year earlier Attilio Bettega had been killed during the same Corsican rally."

The consequences of Toivonen's accident were sudden and far reaching. Within hours FISA President, Jean-Marie Balestre canceled the Group B (and Group S) super car era. The final world championship allowing the use of Group B super cars was The Toyota Olympus Rally in Olympia, Washington, USA, December, 1986.

Only a handful of drivers throughout the world piloted the Group B super cars. John Buffum was one of that elite group.

**JB:** "I don't think the Group B cars were too much for drivers to handle but I do think they were more than we should have been asked to handle. But we were asked and we did it.

They were totally unforgiving. Every rally driver makes errors but the Group B cars did not allow errors. You sometimes just had to be lucky. It wasn't that the drivers weren't competent. On a race track, with a smooth known surface, they were fine. On a gravel road, with things constantly bouncing and the road continuously turning and changing and so much happening at the same time—corners, bumps, ditches, trees, coming at you so quickly—the Group B cars were more than you should ask of a driver.

For instance, Group B cars cut the decision time between corners by one-half from what we were all used to. That also meant a driver's reaction time was cut by one-half.

Recently my stepson's Audi lost its inter-cooler during a rally so he had far less power. But he also had more time. He had to drive faster through corners but he had more time to react and he could notice the difference between the two cars— the difference between 240 hp and 180 hp with the broken inter-cooler—and he could evaluate the corners better because he was coming into them slower.

Now take that equation up to 500 hp or more. People are going to flounder.

I think FISA made the right decision in banning Group B at the time. At some point you have to reign in technology and start again. Eventually the technology will inch back to where it was during the Group B era.

With the ecological ramifications of everything we do these days it's better that we do not use such exotic cars in rallying. The public awareness is much better than it used to be.

Professional rallying is a dangerous sport. We will always have the threat of accidents, injuries and even death. But the super cars raised that threat to a level that was unacceptable.**"**

17.2 A *"Killer Bee"* attacking a stage road on the Nor'wester Pro Rally (Washington). Jon Woodner's Peugeot 205 T-16.

# 18
## Flying Finish
### New World Record

G ILBERT STAEPELAERE WAS born in 1937 in Antwerp, Belgium. His first rally car was a Ford Fairlane V8 in 1954. He drove Fords throughout most of his remarkable rally career, beginning with Anglias in 1960 and ending with Escorts when he retired as an FIA Priority A seeded driver at the end of 1978.

During his career Staepelaere established a new world's record of national championship rally victories—eighty-eight outright wins out of 227 starts. Nineteen of those wins occurred outside his home country.

It was a record that was to stand for nearly eight years.

John Buffum entered his first major rally in 1969, although he did not begin competing seriously until 1973 when the first professional rally championship series was established in North America.

When Buffum retired from full-time active competition at the end of the 1987 season he had posted a new world mark for overall wins on national championship rallies—thirty-four of his major wins occurred outside his home country.

It was an outstanding achievement for an American driver and one that will undoubtedly stand for many years to come. In fact, JB has extended his own world record with several additional victories since 1987.

**JB:** "I think it was sometime in late '85 or early '86 that I first heard of a world's record for national championship victories. Martin Holmes told me the current record of eighty-eight wins was held by a Belgium Ford driver and he reckoned I was getting close to breaking that mark.

I started checking back on my own records and compiling some lists but when I posted my eighty-ninth win at the '86 Nor'wester PRO Rally in Washington State, I didn't even realize I'd already broken the world's record.

*18.1 JB celebrating his 100th championship win and his 44th birthday in 1987.*

I think it really hit home when I won the '87 Ojibwe Rally in Minnesota. My stepson, Paul, Jr., posted a large banner at the victory party, congratulating me on my one hundredth championship win—and my forty-fourth birthday. We all drank a lot of champagne that night.

It was not until some time later I finally figured out the Ojibwe was actually my one hundred and first win—but it didn't matter. That banner was still a special moment. **"**

When the A Priority Rally Driver's seeding list was posted by FISA at the start of the '87 season only twenty-seven international drivers were named, and for the first time ever, an American was included in that ranking of the best rally drivers in the world. John Buffum had earned his A Priority with a third place finish on the 1986 Toyota Olympus International Rally.

To this day he is still the only North American-born driver who has ever gained A Priority status.

**JB:** **"**When Jo Hoppen surprised me by deciding to run the Quattro one final year in 1987, I called Tom to tell him to get ready to go to the opening U.S. event in San Francisco. During that conversation he repeated something he'd said at the start of the '86 season, 'You know, even though its never been done, there is no rule that says we can't win them all.'

I started the year in Canada, winning the Perce Neige with Paul co-driving, then flew to San Francisco for the Barbary Coast PRO Rally—the opening event of the SCCA PRO Rally National Championship Series.

The day before the start the organizers held a press conference during a cruise around San Francisco Bay. The rally (and the cruise) were sponsored by a wine company and we made a serious dent in their annual harvest during the three-hour boat ride. By the time we got in the rental car to drive back to our hotel we were feeling no pain.

And so it was that I began my final championship season by driving into the SCCA National Steward's car while trying to leave the dockside parking lot.

Later that night, after a few more bottles of wine at the welcoming party I got into various arguments with several people about a variety of subjects. I returned to our room and told Grimshaw, 'Well, one good thing happened. At least I pissed off everybody!' I'm not sure what I meant by that but it didn't matter. I fell on my bed and didn't wake up until the following morning.

We were in no shape to start the rally the next day at the Cow Palace and Rod Millen beat us on the opening stage in the parking lot. Then he beat us on the next five spectator stages.

On the final stage of the first day—three laps around a quarter mile race track—I left the track at the end of the second lap even though Tom was yelling, 'No, no, no!' I backed out of the exit road and finished our final lap, then told everyone it was my co-driver's mistake. He'd counted wrong.

We were having a very good time.

Later that night, during dinner, Virginia Reese, head of the SCCA PRO Rally Board and a co-driver on the Subaru team, stopped by our table and accused us of not being serious about the rally. She was right, and I think she was a bit worried. She'd been co-driving for Ola Stromberg, the Swedish National Champion, when they passed by the scene of our bad crash in Pennsylvania in '85. She'd also been in several bad crashes herself and knew first hand what could happen at the speeds we were running if we weren't really concentrating.

The next day the rally went into the mountains and I went to work, built up a four-minute lead and coasted home in first place overall.

So much for not trying. **"**

**T**he Group B super cars had been banned from international competition beginning in 1987, but were still allowed in many national series—including those in North America. Buffum had expected to get a new Group A Audi Quattro Coupe early in the year but it didn't arrive until just before the Olympus World Championship Rally in late June.

Rod Millen retired his all-wheel-drive Mazda RX-7 after the Barbary Coast Rally and ran a Group A Mazda 323 for the rest of the season. The change did only slowed him somewhat and he dogged JB's heels throughout the year.

By June Buffum had won the first three rounds of the U.S.championship series and had also won his only start in the Canadian national series. He was well on his way to repeating as U.S. and North American Rally Cup champion.

**JB:** "I got our Group A Coupe Quattro in early June and took it to the Olympus WCR in the last week of the month. Tom and I had gone out early to do the pacenotes and Neil Wilson again came over to co-drive for me while Tom rode with Paul, Jr., in the Group N 4000S Quattro.

The first time Neil and I practiced in Washington in the Group A car I told the guys 'This thing is a real dog.' I felt it was way too slow, that something was wrong with it. I even called Germany to ask if something could be done to increase its speed and asked some other drivers to try it to see what they thought. Of course nothing was wrong with the car—it was just the difference between 200 hp and 500 hp. It was just like Martin Holmes wrote about Group A at the start of 1987, 'Drivers will have to relearn the skill of mechanical sympathy rather than saving split seconds.'

The '87 Olympus was once more the most important rally ever held in the United States. In '86 it had been a driver-points-only world championship rally but in '87 it was a full-fledged manufacturer's and driver's points event. It drew the best drivers in international rallying and lasted five days.

209

Paul and Tom lasted two days. Neil and I lasted three.

During the first night the dust was horrible, even with the aid of pacenotes. Paul caught a tree on the co-driver's side and when the car stopped spinning in the dust neither he nor Tom knew which way they should go. They had to back off the road and wait for the following car to show them which way the stage went. The service crew kept the car going until the next night but it was in pretty bad shape and Paul pulled out at the next overnight halt.

Neil and I were doing fairly well by the third day as I was trying to learn how to drive the slower Group A car for the first time. Then, with the sun directly in my eyes, a miscommunication on a pacenote caused a serious crash in which we rolled several times. It was the end of our rally.

The next day about a dozen of us took a couple cars and drove up into Mount Rainier National Park to look at the mountain. The rally was still going on but by then we didn't give a damn. It was a beautiful day. We loaded up the coolers and went sightseeing and had a very good time.

Juha Kankkunen won the Olympus by twelve seconds over Miki Biasion with Markku Alen finishing third. All three were driving Group A Lancia Delta HF 4WDs. Kankkunen went on to win the world championship in 1987—the first-ever rally driver to win the international championship two years in a row.

We went home and prepared to resume the PRO Rally season. **"**

JB used the short wheel-base Group B Quattro to win the next two U.S. events—the Sunriser 400 in Columbus, Ohio and the Ojibwe in Grand Rapids, Minnesota. He also took two more wins in Canada: The Dyfi Ste. Agathe with Grimshaw and the Voyager with his stepson, Paul, in the rebuilt Group A

Coupe. It was the fourth year in a row he and Grimshaw had won The Dyfi in St. Agathe, Quebec.

In September he took a weekend away from rallying and returned to the race track, joining Jon Woodner and Jeff Andretti to win SSA in an Audi 5000 Quattro at the Mid-Ohio Escort 24-Hour race.

**JB:** "Tom and I had a funny moment during the Sunriser 400. We had about a four-minute lead when we hit a patch of broken tarmac on a hard down hill righthander and slid straight off into a large open pit. The car was pointing almost straight down with the brakes locked when Tom jumped out to get some spectators to help us.

I threw the car into reverse, revved the hell out of it, let off the brake and popped out of the hole and flew backwards across the road, through a ditch and into the woods. It happened so fast I wasn't sure what was in front of me and I started yelling at Grimshaw to see if I could safely move forward. Meanwhile he was gathering up people to push me out of the woods. I got really frustrated because he wouldn't answer me and I was banging on the steering wheel and yelling. Finally I just put it into gear and drove out onto the road. Tom jumped in and away we went.

Later we realized that there was no way he could have heard me. The car was making a hell of a noise, he was outside wearing a helmet, yelling at people, I was inside with the doors closed, wearing a helmet, yelling at him, revving the engine— no way.

We laughed about it later. What was a little yelling among good friends?"

When Buffum and Grimshaw won the POR (the toughest rally in the U.S.) in Michigan in late October with the Sport Quattro, Paul Choiniere, Jr., and Scott Weinheimer finished third overall behind them and won Group A honors in JB's Audi

211

Coupe. The four teammates celebrated at the finish line with several bottles of champagne as they sat on top of the winning Audi for a group photo.

Later at the victory party, JB announced his retirement from full-time competition at the end of the current season.

Two weeks later, following his win on the final U.S. championship event of 1987, the Wild West PRO Rally in Olympia, Washington, the organizers held a farewell banquet to honor one of their own—the most successful professional rally driver in North America.

After several competitors spoke of his accomplishments (and detailed many of his faults in a good natured roasting), John Buffum spoke for the last time as the current rally champion of the United States.

It had been twelve years since his first major championship win. In that span of time he established a new world record of 105 overall wins on national championship rallies. He won twelve U.S. national championships (eleven SCCA titles and one NARRA title), nine North American Rally Cup championships and six manufacturer's championships. He'd been named three times to the American Auto Racing Writers & Broadcasters Association All American Racing Team and had set new records at the famed Pikes Peak Auto Hill Climb.

And to top off his amazing career, John Buffum won every national championship rally he ran in the U.S. and Canada in 1987, the only time that feat has ever been accomplished.

It was a fitting end to an illustrious career.

His final victory in 1987 took place in the bitter cold of Canada where he won the Tall Pines Rally in Peterborough, Ontario, driving a Group A 4000S Audi Quattro.

It was not the final time he and his co-driver, Tom Grimshaw, would win a rally together but it was the last time they would win as full-time professionals.

The following morning the two friends shook hands in the ice-covered parking lot and when they parted, John Buffum's years as a professional rally driver—perhaps the best there will ever be in North America—came to an end.

He went out the same way he tells young drivers to come out of the corners . . . LIKE A LION!

*18.2 1987: The Perfect Year. JB and Tom Grimshaw celebrate their POR victory atop the Audi Group B Sport Quattro. Their teammates, Paul Choiniere, Jr. (R) and Scott Weinheimer (L), winners of Group A, join the party. Note the "no smoking" and "wheelchair" emblems on Grimshaw's window. (Photo: Trackside Photo, Inc.)*

*18.3 John Buffum—OUT LIKE A LION. (Photo: Colin Taylor Productions)*

# PART FOUR

*JB begins his 1982 record breaking "race to the clouds" up Pikes Peak.*

# 19

# Race to the Clouds
## King of the Hill

O NE HUNDRED AND EIGHTY-SIX YEARS ago an army lieutenant with the unlikely name of Zebulon Montgomery Pike was the first white man to ever see the Colorado mountain that was later to bear his name. In 1806 he declared that "Pikes Peak" would never be climbed.

Seventy-four years later, in 1880, a carriage road was built to the summit of Lieutenant Pike's mountain. Another twenty-two years would pass before an automobile would reach the 14,110 foot peak. The climb was made by two Denver men, Yont and Felker, in a two-cylinder Locomobile Steamer. The car was driven halfway up and pushed the rest of the way. The climb took nine hours—the first unofficial Pikes Peak Hill Climb record.

In 1915, Spencer Penrose, a wealthy Colorado Springs philanthropist, decided that driving up Pikes Peak could be a major tourist attraction. He spent half a million dollars constructing the road that is still used today. At that time it was the world's highest auto highway.

Penrose introduced his new toll road to the public in 1916 by staging the first Pikes Peak Auto Hill Climb. It was won by twenty-two year old Rea Lentz in an open cockpit Romano Demon Special—the smallest car in the field. His winning time was twenty minutes, 55.6 seconds. Barney Oldfield was listed among the losers.

During the following years the unique mountain climb became a legend in American racing lore. Third only to the Mount Washington Hill Climb and the Indy 500 in longevity and popularity, the annual "Race To The Clouds" attracted world-wide interest and its list of champions read like a "Who's Who In Auto Racing": Mario Andretti, Roger and Rick Mears, Curtis Turner, Parnelli Jones and many, many others, including the Unser family—kings of the mountain.

The Unsers—Louis, Bobby, Al, Jerry, Bobby Jr., Al Jr. and Robby—dominate the Pikes Peak record books dating back to 1934. The family has won the event twenty-three times!

By 1981 popularity of the historic race, then sanctioned by USAC, was on the wane. It did not offer the allure of past years and the press had grown tired of writing the same trite praises year after year.

The Pikes Peak Auto Hill Climb needed something new.

At that same time the SCCA was seeking ways to publicize its growing PRO Rally Series. Terry Moreland, SCCA Rally Manager, received a telephone call from Charles Tutt, President of the Pikes Peak Hill Climb Association.

"Would SCCA be interested in sanctioning the Pikes Peak Auto Hill Climb?" inquired Tutt.

"Yes," Moreland answered, "But only if you add a new class for our rally cars."

It was a marriage made in heaven—or at least in the clouds atop the summit of Pikes Peak—close enough.

Introduction of the "Rally Division" in 1981 was a ho-hum affair and was met with some resentment and derision by the hard-core hill climbers. Five rally cars raced up the mountain, running at the end of the line when most spectators were packing up to leave and most media coverage had ended for the day. Dan Hoffpauir won the new class in a two-seat Wells Coyote open wheel roadster that had never before appeared in a rally. The first true rally car, a Mazda RX-7, driven by New Zealander, John Woolf, finished five seconds behind Hoffpauir.

218

It was a sorry beginning for the new rally division and did little to enhance either the race or professional rallying in the U.S.

But what it did do was attract the attention of Josef Hoppen, the guiding force behind Porsche-Audi's U.S. competition department.

Hoppen telephoned his rally driver, John Buffum . . . .

**JB:** "In 1982, Jo Hoppen, with great foresight, decided to send me to Pikes Peak with the same Audi Quattro I was using in the SCCA PRO Rally Series. He brought Audi's engine man, Mike Rossman, over from Germany to help us sort out the fuel injection and turbo systems. Another wise move.

The race starts at 9,402 feet above sea level and finishes at 14,110 feet. There are 156 corners over 12.42 miles of hardpacked clay and gravel surfaced public road. Fuel management in the thin mountain air was extremely important if I was to do anything with a 330 hp production-based car.

We got three days of practice on the hill, one-third of the course each day, beginning at 6:00 A.M. and ending at 8:00 A.M.,when the road was opened to the public. We got about three runs a day but there was really no way I could tell how I'd do until I ran the full course on race day.

After our practice sessions ended each morning I'd spend the rest of the day playing golf at the Air Force Academy with Colonel Edwin (Bish) Bishop who was my father's best friend and served with him in Panama during World War II.

Mike Rossman rode with me on several practice runs, checking his instruments, making notes, fiddling with the fuel injection system and measuring the revolutions of the turbo as the elevation increased each day.

My main competition that year was Scott Harvey in a beefed up 4WD '79 Dodge Aspen and Jon Woodner in a Triumph TR-8, both very good rally drivers with a lot of racing experience.

219

On Thursday we made a single qualifying run from the start to Glen Cove, about halfway up the mountain. The weather was just perfect. Woodner set fastest time for our division. I apexed a corner too tight, hit a berm and knocked a turbo hose off. I was doing 10 mph at the finish—the slowest qualifier in our class.

Finally race day came and I admit I was a bit nervous, not nearly as calm as I am at the start of a rally stage. It wasn't the exposures or the high elevations, it was the realization that I'd only get one shot at it. One run. If I messed it up, spun out or blew a turn . . . I'd lose. Running Pikes Peak is like jamming all the stages of a rally into one single stage. Twelve miles and you only get one try. It's not a particularly frightening run but there are two left handers after you go up through the 'W's, past Devil's Playground, that are 'daunting' because you have no point of reference. It's all blue sky out the window shield and that makes it very difficult.

The rules allow the fastest qualifiers to pick their starting positions within their division on race day. Most of the fastest drivers try to start at the rear of their group so the front runners will brush the loose gravel off the corners and give them better traction. But in our division, since we were the last cars to run, our fast guys ran at the head of our group because they didn't want to be last car up the mountain, when everyone was getting ready to leave.

There was a motorcycle class that year and they'd had a big pile-up that killed one rider, so the course was closed for quite some time. By the time the ambulances cleared the road and the rally cars got to start it was very late in the day. KRDO Radio of Colorado Springs covered the race and their broadcast ended at 5:00 P.M.—about five minutes after my start time. So they were off the air before I finished my run.

Cars usually start about one or two minutes apart to make sure there's no passing on the way up. Catching another car is very rare unless there's been a breakdown or something unusual happens. Ralph Starr started in front of me and I was

*19-1 1982: JB waits at the top of Pikes Peak while Audi's engine man, Mike Rossman, works magic on the Audi Quattro during practice.*

held five minutes to make sure I wouldn't overtake him . . . but I passed him two-thirds of the way up.

When I crossed the finish line at the summit I felt I'd had a good run. I'd driven well and the Audi, thanks to Mike Rossman's expertise, had run just great. I waited in the car for my time to be announced. I really had no idea how I compared to the rest of the field.

I waited and waited and finally, after about five minutes, I asked if there was a problem. No one was saying anything to me. In fact, they were obviously ignoring me.

I was told the officials couldn't believe my time and were verifying it—double checking everything.

221

When they finally announced my time—12 minutes, 20.52 seconds—it was a new record."

**N**ot only had Buffum shattered the previous rally division record by nearly a full minute, he beat the Stock Car Division record by thirty seconds! Only eight cars in the super fast, specialty-built Open Wheel Division beat JB's time.

Needless to say, he was voted "Rookie of the Year."

Suddenly the motoring press and the rest of the world sat up and took notice. A little German built "rally" sedan had just set new records in Colorado. The Pikes Peak Auto Hill Climb was once again big news, both in the U.S. and across the Atlantic.

JB returned to Pikes Peak in 1983 and easily won the rally division despite the absence of technical assistance from the Audi factory.

Michael Jordan's article in the October, 1983 issue of *Car and Driver* magazine, titled "Quattro On The Mountain," best described JB's 1983 drive:

"Buffum has a few things in his favor. First, he has an uncanny memory for roads, a talent exhibited publicly only in extremely precise and complex directions in neighborhood pubs.

"Second, Buffum is a rally driver and this sport develops a driver's judgment and car control to levels rarely seen in other forms of racing; indeed, rally drivers might be the best race drivers in the world.

"It is roughly one-hundred yards from the point where the cars start to the point where the timer is triggered; Buffum is in third gear as the clocks are tripped. By the first corner, another one-hundred yards away, Buffum is already in fifth gear. The car looks tentative compared with the graceful sliding Chevette V-6 driven by the thoughtful and talented Kiwi immigrant Clive Smith, but Buffum is merely maximizing traction.

"On and off, on and off. Traction is getting power to the ground, not pressing through the limit. Wheelspin is not speed," he likes to say. Buffum dodges a man chasing a dog across the road and then nearly puts a wheel across the forehead of a photographer hiding in a ditch. At Glen Cove, the halfway point, the turbo boost is reading 1.5 bars, less than he would like.

"The road from Glen Cove to the ridge line climbs several thousand feet in just three miles through switchbacks called Ws. At the last W at the top of the grade, the spectators in the Devil's Playground get a close-up of the Quattro's capabilities. Buffum screams past the braking point used by all the open-wheelers, bearing down on a couple of film crews brazenly cranking away on the outside of the left-hand hairpin. A ripple of interest stirs through the crowd: this guy is going to crash for sure; and if he does go off, he'll starve to death before he hits bottom.

Buffum bangs the brakes so hard his Comp T/As actually chirp on the dirt. Then he wiggles the car toward the right—toward the precipice. Three onlookers on that side of the road chicken out and jump off the mountain to get out of the way of the crash. Then Buffum flings the wheel to the left again, and in classic style, the back of the Quattro swings around to the right, gracefully pivoting the car. Then the Quattro pelts up the hill at 7000 rpm, past an inscription some wag has scrawled in the snow over-hanging the road. It reads, 'Quattro rules.'

At the top of the mountain, Buffum lets the Quattro loose for the three-mile sprint to the finish, ignoring the two guys sauntering across the road, disdainful of the blue sky that borders most of the curves and hopeful that his turbo will prove to be an advantage at an altitude that cuts the power of a naturally aspirated stock-block engine in half.

"At the finish, it's clear that Buffum and Quattro have done it again. All the stock cars have been vanquished, and the Quattro is right up there with the open-wheelers–sixth fastest overall, in fact.

"There's one difference this year, everyone is glad to see him win. Al Unser, Jr. comes over and graciously compliments Buffum on his skill and the capability of his car. The officials shake his hand. And why not . . . he, his crew and his car are now part of the Pikes Peak legend, not a threat to it."

**D**uring the next four years Audi continued to dominate the rally division, and ultimately, the entire field, despite heavy competition from other European manufacturers who were suddenly flocking to Colorado in July.

**JB:** "In 1984 Audi sent me back to Pikes Peak to work as a liaison with their factory driver, Michele Mouton, in her attempt to break the overall hill record. Michele had come within one event of becoming the world champion in 1982. She'd won several world championship rallies for Audi and was used to high pressure situations. But she upset the organizers at the hill climb and they were more than eager to put a female upstart in her place.

The trouble started when she was moving the Quattro to the start line for her qualifying run. She smoked the tires to heat them up. That pissed everybody off. The organizers fined her and would not allow her to drive the car except from the start line to the top of the mountain—nowhere else!

I had to drive the car to the start line. Then I'd get out and Michele would get in and race up the hill. On race day, the mechanics had to push the car to the start line before Michele was allowed in the driver's seat.

She easily won the rally class that year but missed the overall record.

The entire affair had to be very embarrassing for her. However, later that night she was in better humor at a sit down Audi dinner as she explained to me the origin of a certain expletive which is the shorthand version of 'Fornicate Under Command of the King.'

Michele Mouton returned in 1985, with fire in her eyes, and destroyed all the good ol' boys' long cherished traditions of the Pikes Peak Auto Hill Climb.

First she announced she'd like to take her co-driver, Fabrizia Pons, with her during the actual race. Officials rushed to their rule books and found they had never covered that eventuality. Fabrizia did ride on some practice runs but not on race day.

Then she not only won the rally division for her second year in a row, she set a new overall hill record.

Perhaps the old guard on the hill should have taken heed of *Car and Driver's* implied warning when they named her one of the ten best race drivers in the world.

Michele was not overly popular with the heavy-metal stock car and open-wheeler specialty boys who owned Pikes Peak before the rally cars arrived at the start line in 1981. First, she was a woman. Second, she was a foreigner. Third, she drove a foreign car. And fourth, she drove a rally car, of all damned things! What was the world coming to?**"**

It was coming back to the Unser family.

In 1986, Audi joined forces with Bobby Unser who had twelve previous overall victories on the mountain and, in 1982, had been elected "Honorary Lifetime Director" of the Pikes Peak Hill Climb Association.

John Buffum was sent back to Colorado as an advisor . . . .

**JB:** "I have the greatest admiration for Bobby Unser. He's a great Indy car racer, but in 1986 he was a horse's ass at Pikes Peak. I'm not really sure what a horse's ass is, but what ever it is, he was it!

That year Audi sent over its newest S1 Sport Quattro, known in America as the "Batmobile" because of its radical styling and awesome power. Much of the shell was made of very light-weight Kevlar and its engine put out more than 600 hp.

I felt the same way Walter Rohrl felt years before, when he was driving for Lancia and tested Michele Mouton's Quattro. He said, 'Even a monkey could drive this car and win.'

Bobby Unser had gone to Germany to learn about driving the car from the factory expert, two-time world rally champion, Walter Rohrl. Then they sent me to Colorado to work with the team before the race.

During testing and practice Bobby totally screwed up a winning rally car that, at that time, was dominating everything in the world. He removed all the good pieces, took out the electric clutch, eliminated the pre-loading in the rear diff, changed springs and shocks, etc. I think he was trying to live up to his reputation, his image of dialing in his cars to suit his driving style. But it just said to me that if he had driven Indy cars that were properly set up, he could have won even more races than he did during his career. I believe his exceptional driving abilities overcame the less than perfect setups on his cars.

At least it did for sure at Pikes Peak in 1986 when he still won and set a new record in a car he had messed up with his meddling."

A year later, Audi sent Walter Rohrl to the mountain with a newer version of the S1 Sport Quattro and he broke Unser's record, but that was to be the end of Audi's domination of the hill.

The following year, Ari Vatanen, also a past world rally

*19.2 1986: Bobby Unser driving the Audi Quattro "Batmobile" to a new Pikes Peak Auto Hill Climb record. (Photo: Su Kemper)*

champion, took the title away from Audi and set a new overall record of 10 minutes, 47.22 seconds in a 405 T16 Peugeot—a rally car. He beat Rohrl's record by a mere 0.63 seconds!

And finally, in 1989, a young man named Robby Unser won the race in a Peugeot 405 Turbo 16 4WS, but barely missed Vatanen's overall record despite the addition of four-wheel-steering. Still, he did set a new record that was probably more important to the young race driver—he was the fastest Unser to ever climb Pikes Peak.

Today, the rally division still holds the overall record for the famed Pikes Peak Auto Hill Climb, but it all began in 1982, when John Buffum drove a rally car up the mountain so fast the officials could not believe his time.

That was the true beginning of the new era of "racing to the clouds."

# 20
## Germany in the Snow
### Hired Gun

**J B** : "ON A SNOWY MORNING in January, 1983, I was backing my street Quattro out of the driveway when my wife Mary yelled for me to wait because I had a call from Germany. So I left the car running, thinking I'd only be a couple of minutes and it usually didn't roll at all so I didn't set the hand brake.

I left the driver's door open and ran into the house. When I returned, the car had rolled backwards and crunched its door on the bumper of Mary's car.

That's how I remember the telephone call that took me to West Germany a few weeks later. I was already bending cars and I hadn't even left for the rally yet.

The call was from Konrad Schmidt, the German tuner who was entrusted with the Audi Quattros in the German National Championship series. Audi Sport was running the World Championships and they allowed national importers to run their individual national series with a combined budget. Like Libra Racing in the U.S., Schmidt Motorsport was the contact in Germany. He was only about forty-five minutes from Audi's headquarters in Inglestodt.

During the telephone call Herr Schmidt told me their own team driver, Harald Demuth (1982 German rally champion), was not available for the Sachs Winter Rally in Germany, and asked if I would come over and drive their Quattro with their team co-driver, Arwed Fischer. Even though Demuth couldn't run, Audi could still get manufacturer's points so they wanted to enter the car.

I don't know why they called me. But, in retrospect, I guess there just weren't many qualified Quattro drivers around back then. He offered me a fee, around $200 a day, and expenses. This wasn't a world championship rally, but it was a European and German national championship rally. A co-efficient two event.

So I went to Germany in February.

I arrived a week early and met Arwed Fischer. We picked up a Quattro street car from Audi Sport and drove up to the course in northeastern Germany, right along the East German border. In fact, we ran about one hundred-feet from the border on one transit. We could see the guards in their lookout towers, the machine-guns, the barbed wire, and the no-man's land full of minefields. At one place the border cut right through a small town and the barbed wire ran between two houses.

We practiced and took pacenotes for three days. I'd never met Fischer before but I knew he spoke English and we agreed to use the same type of English notes I was used to.

The stages consisted of a wide variety of roads and we didn't know if we'd have snow or no snow during the two day rally. Germany is not like Vermont. Its weather is more like Ohio or Michigan. Some of the stages were just bare asphalt and some were totally covered in ice and snow, and some were a combination of conditions. It made tire selection very difficult.

The best roads in Germany are in the forests but organizers have great trouble getting permission to use them. As I understood it, in 1972 and '73 they had a big rally called The Olympia Rally, and they used all the good forest roads—but never had official permission to do so. It pissed off the forestry

230

and government people so they banned rallies from the forests.

Stage roads for the German championship rallies were reasonable but sort of put-together things. We'd run down an asphalt road for three or four kilometers, then turn onto a very small two-track narrow trail through the woods, then turn again at a crossroad and come out on a much faster gravel road.

I remarked to Arwed how good the stage roads were in the U.S. compared to any you find in the rest of the world, at least in all the places I'd been, and that the German roads were not nearly as nice as ours.

For instance, in England, the roads in Kielder are crummy. Wales has some excellent stages and the Lake District and Scotland have some nice sections. But 50 percent of the stages in England are not nearly as good as those in the U.S.

On world championship rallies, some of the roads are just plain flat-ass rough. The Acropolis is extremely rough. Costa Smeralda has beautiful stages—the nicest rally of any I did outside North America. Portugal—I didn't do a rally there but I did do some testing for Audi and many of their roads are not very good.

Stage roads in the United States compare very favorably with the rest of the world.

During practice we drove all day and made our notes, then stayed in little German hotels at night. We rarely saw anyone during the day but at night we'd meet several competitors in the hotel bars. Many of them spoke English when they talked to me, but they'd ask Arwed a lot of questions about me in German. They wondered if I was the same American who had done the Monte Carlo Rallye and other German rallies fifteen years earlier. They also kept asking if I knew how to drive on snow and ice. They didn't know I was from Vermont, or they didn't know what winters were like in Vermont.

Arwed told them, yes, he can drive on snow. It wasn't the answer they wanted to hear . . . but they were quite nice to me anyway.

The rally started in Bad Harzburg and returned there the first day. Then it went to Hanover and finished in Hamburg, at a major VW plant. The press later wrote there were approximately 80,000 spectators over the two days.

The German people are very intelligent and well informed rally spectators. They know where to go for the action. Lots of stages had several thousand people spectating. There wasn't much crowd control, but not much was required because they were very well behaved; not like the Mediterranean area where they're just plain crazy.

The opening stage was about ten kilometers, up and down hills in the trees. It was a public-type road with a guardrail. On the way up, there were patches of snow and on the way down, on the sunny side, there wasn't any snow at all, so choice of tires was very tough. We used wide M&S Pirellis on the first stage, but they had servicing between every stage and Schmidt had one of his guys running ahead of the rally, trying to let us know the road conditions. We made a lot of tire changes; most good and a few not so good.

For some unknown reason I was seeded number one on the very first European Championship rally I'd run in a competitive car. I wondered what Walter Smolej, Erwin Weber or Kalle Grundel thought about that. They were all factory drivers with very good winning records. Smolej drove a Ford Escort RS. Weber was in an Opel Ascona 400. Grundel was an ex-fighter pilot who later ran for VW on world championship rallies. He was driving a German importer's VW Golf GTI.

I was a bit nervous at the start. I made the first few corners okay then I came into one far too fast and just barely made it around. I don't think Arwed knew but I said to myself 'careful, you asshole.' Sometimes, in a Quattro, on pacenotes, you think you're invincible. I was a bit more careful from then on.

We won the opening stage by a few seconds and no one ever caught us again.

Later I passed both Weber and Grundel when they stuffed into a snow bank on one of the stages where we did several loops.

The condition of the roads changed between the time we did our notes and when we ran the rally. During practice we met people cross-country skiing on one stage so we knew it would be covered in snow at rally time. One stage was about five or six miles around a farmer's asphalt cart path, but with a two-hundred yard stretch of snow-covered gravel linking the sections. We did three laps on that road and used intermediate racing tires, so when we turned off on the connecting road, at a narrow Tee-junction, we had to be very careful because braking on the snow with racing tires was really dodgey.

One stage was scrubbed because there were too many tourists present. Another had been changed since we made our notes. It was a short three or four miler. At one point out pacenotes said turn left, but during the rally it was barricaded so we had to turn the other way and finish the stage with no notes.

We mounted M&S tires on a stage that began on wet pavement, ran onto gravel, then onto a short section of snow and ice. I didn't like the tire choice. There was a fast left around a hill with a field on the outside, on gravel, and I slid the Quattro totally off, into a field, but kept the power on and came back onto the road. Then in the snow, at a crossroad left, the rear came out and kissed the bank. I caught it again. It was the only tire choice I thought was wrong. The crew picked them for the asphalt and didn't give enough regard to the slippery gravel and snow.

At one point, after I had 'attacked' a few corners, gotten sloppy, and slid wide several times, Arwed told me to ease up

233

a bit and use the advantage of four-wheel-drive. Don't over drive the car. Stay steady. Not too fast. Use good braking going in, don't worry about going around the corner so fast, then use the acceleration from the power and 4WD to come out—use it!

He was right. I had to let the car help me win the rally. I didn't need to win it in the corners.

IN LIKE A LAMB, OUT LIKE A LION!

I still tell young drivers that same thing today. Get in there, get through, get set up, and get the power on early.

Arwed was very good with the notes. He also set up all the service points and they worked very well. All the technical stuff went very good.

There wasn't a lot of interaction with the other drivers, even after I took the lead right from the start. I think they had found out I was the U.S. champion, but until then an American had never won a European championship rally. I didn't speak a lot of German so Arwed would get out during the longer pauses and talk to the other teams. I was just the foreign professional hired gun brought in to do a job, and when it was over I'd go home.

I didn't know what reaction the press would have.

On the second and final day I had more confidence. We had about a minute and a half lead. Not blowing anyone away, just going along steady, very workmanlike. Seeing how things would go.

No one really took a run at me. We'd just stay with them on the asphalt and beat them on the snowy gravel sections, using the four-wheel-drive of the Quattro.

The final stage was a very fast straight asphalt road with two hay-bale chicanes built into it. Then it went off into a small muddy gravel pit section. We had to do three laps around it.

There was a bit of animosity between Arwed Fischer on the Audi team and the guys on the Opel team. They were year-long combatants.

234

On the second lap we saw Erwin Weber in front of us in his Opel Ascona and Arwed said, 'Go get him.' So I really started trying extra hard and caught him at the top of a little rise in front of a lot of spectators. I passed him on the inside. Fischer loved it.

Then I caught Grundel and I was a bit more careful. I followed him through part of a gravel pit until he finally let me by but while I was following him he covered my driving lights with mud. Since it had just turned dark, I couldn't see a thing once I passed him.

Then Smolej caught me on the asphalt during the final lap. He was running in second place, less than two minutes behind us and he'd just put a full minute on us. So I knew I had to hold him off until we went back into the shit where he couldn't pass me.

At the hay-bale chicanes he was right on my tail and when we came out I used every bit of power I could. Then he came right up again on the next two corners before we went into the muddy bit and I sprayed shit all over his lights and blinded him.

At the final finish control I could tell he was really pissed off when he came over. He claimed I blocked him and wouldn't let him by. He was shouting in German and I wasn't sure what he was saying exactly, so I just sort of shrugged and said, 'I don't understand, what's the matter?'

Of course I knew damned well what he was shouting about. I'd held him off. I wasn't about to let him by—but I also wasn't about to tell him that right then.

After a while he calmed down and realized it's all part of the sport of stage rallying.

We beat Smolej by fifty-eight seconds and Weber by seven and a half minutes. Grundel finished well down in ninth place, fourteen minutes behind us.

235

It was a great win for Audi Germany. We sat on top of the car at the finish and sprayed champagne on everyone and drank a good share of it. There was a very big crowd cheering us. Audi is a German company and they really wanted to win in their own country, so everyone was very pleased.

I was the first American driver to ever win a European championship rally! (Today I'm still the only American driver to ever win any European championship rallies.)

Back home it was as if nothing had happened. I took my helmet to Germany and I brought my helmet home. Just another day's work!**"**

# 21

## The Major Leagues
### Victory In Cyprus

*I*N 1984 JOHN BUFFUM, with backing from BFGoodrich, Hella lights and Audi Sport, competed in five major European rallies. He drove 15,000 miles practicing, 2,000 miles at speed on stages, flew more than 60,000 miles—just in Europe. In addition, he did nine national championship events in the U.S. and two in Canada.

He spent 140 days on the road . . . .

**JB:** "During 1983 I had several talks with the people from BFGoodrich about doing a program in Europe with an Audi Quattro. They wanted to expand their sales overseas and had already done some other things with me outside the U.S. When I ran the Triumph in Europe in 1981 BFG had done the press announcements and painted the car and did some other good stuff with their dealers.

So in 1983 I decided I wanted to do a European program the following year. I wrote Konrad Schmidt in Germany and David Sutton in England. I knew Schmidt from the Sachs Winter Rally in '83 and Sutton had been preparing world-class rally cars for many years and was currently managing the Audi efforts in England.

I asked for quotes on eight events and Schmidt came back with a bid of $400,000 U.S. currency, compared to Sutton's $320,000.

We'd heard a bit of talk that Sutton was not always exactly straight . . . like after you shook hands you'd better count your fingers. But he had a reputation of being very professional and he'd done an excellent job running the World Championship Ford teams in the past. Still, we heard the rumors; he was a businessman first and foremost and might shave a few corners here and there for sake of the bottom line.

After seeing the cost of eight events we decided to drop back to five; Costa Smeralda (Sardinia), Acropolis (Greece), Hunsruck (Germany), Cyprus (Cyprus), and RAC (England).

Sutton came back with a new price of 120,000 £ He was to build the car (which belonged to him), transport and maintain it, provide service during the rallies—cover everything except practice and driver/co-driver expenses.

I added $60,000 to cover my costs. My fee was about $30,000, out of which I gave $5,000 to the co-drivers. I had to cover our expenses, shipping costs for tires ($12,000), painting costs for the car, and other miscellaneous items. I also included expenses for taking my own mechanic, 'Salty,' to all five events.

Then, after I finalized the deal with BFG, I got a lucky break. Sutton's quote was in British pounds and the pound dropped in value so I picked up about $15,000 profit in the exchange rate.

BFGoodrich's portion of the program was to cover all the promotional things. I don't know what their total budget was but they got ESPN-TV to come over with us and most of the World Championship rallies were shown back in the U.S. on ESPN.

The apprehension about David Sutton turned out to be no problem at all. He was a quality guy with a quality operation. He was right there all the time and did everything he was supposed to do and did them very well. And he provided excellent service crews.

238

There was a time in Greece at the Acropolis when we were sitting seventh overall and he bought a lot of new spare parts from Audi Sport to make sure we had enough. First-class all the way.

Of course, Sutton also may have had his reservations. We did the first rally at Costa Smeralda and I went off and smashed the rear of the car. Then Salty, trying to catch up somewhere, lost the chase car going too fast into a curve and bashed in the side bouncing off several stone kilometer markers.

So Sutton takes two wrecked cars back to England after the very first rally and I could just picture him sitting at home thinking, *Boy this is going to be a very long and very expensive year.*"

John Buffum's diary covering the five European rallies in 1984 was reported by journalist, Tim Cline, *Road & Track* magazine:

Event: Costa Smeralda
Series: European Championship
Headquarters: Perto Cervo, Sardinia, Italy
Date: April 26-28, 1984
Length: 1,264 km. (stages: 43—650 km.)
Co-driver: Neil Wilson
Result: DNF—accident, Stage Thirteen

### Perto Cervo, Sardinia, Italy (April 29, Reuters)

Finnish rally sensation Henri Toivonen drove his Rothman's Porsche 911SC/RS to a one-minute win over Italian Carlo Capone's Lancia 037 at the Costa Smeralda Rally. The win moved Toivonen to within striking distance of Capone who still holds the lead in the European Rally Championship after fifteen events. Toivonen spent all of the time outside the car hobbling around on crutches as a result of a karting accident a week earlier in Ireland. Several of the favorite Italian teams crashed out early in the event and Adartico Vudafieri, who let most of the event in his Totip Lancia 037, retired on Stage Thirty-eight when the car's engine blew. American John Buffum crashed his BF Goodrich Audi Quattro early in the event, while lying seventh.

JB: Maybe I should find a different line of work. I am also beginning to wonder if agreeing to do this article (and keep this diary) was such a good idea. The reason is sitting twenty feet from me—my smashed Quattro. What do you say about driving and crashing, not once, but twice before the event even got going good? Maybe it wouldn't be so bad if so many of the other cars hadn't dropped out or had trouble. I think we had a shot at a top-three finish; instead we have a broken rally car. Not only that, but the crew also crashed the chase car. Sutton must be wondering what he got himself into. One event and two crashed cars—great start for a racing season.

We had left the states on a sour note anyway, after the U.S. Quattro lost its engine at the Olympus PRO Rally in Washington and we hadn't finished. Salty Sottolano, my chief mechanic, and I flew to Rome and then on to Sardinia for Costa Smeralda. Because I had run this event a few times before and I had a good finish here, I was looking forward to it. Neil Wilson, my co-driver for this event, and I, had spent a week in late March on Sardinia practicing and making pace notes.

The rally itself is most civilized, running from 9:00 A.M. to late evening for three days. Our trouble started about ten kilometers into the second stage. At a slight right over a crest, the road narrowed a bit and there were stone walls on both sides. I was using all the road; so when

240

the road narrowed, there was nowhere to go and we hit the wall, bam! We rapped the left rear of the car and spun 180 degrees. The car skidded to a halt backward down the stage, between the stone walls. There was stone wall all over the road. We got going and turned around, but there was obviously something very wrong with the left rear of the car. We were driving slowly, just trying to make it to the end of the stage.

A few kilometers later, we came to this fast sweeping left just in time to see a helicopter taking off and all the cars that were ahead of us stopped on the road. Attiligo Bettega, driving the number-one car (a Lancia) had understeered off the road and hit a stone face on the co-driver's side of the car. The co-driver had broken one or both of his legs and was being medivac'ed to a hospital. That was quick work because we were only five or six minutes behind Bettega. It meant that the stage had to be canceled, so our little accident would not hurt our score at all.

*Well*, I thought, *it looks like we dodged the bullet.*

Fat chance. Stage Thirteen was the first night stage, and the dust was really getting bad. I got wide on a right-hander and hit a rock ledge at about 75 or 80 mph. It must have thrown us ten feet in the air. The car spun in mid-air and landed on the right rear. We had dislodged this huge boulder, and the car was absolutely dead because the impact had knocked the master switch off. So there we were in the dark and dust; and we could just picture the next car coming out of the dust straight at us. I got the car restarted and sort of shuffled over behind the big boulder and turned the lights on.

This was not exactly what I had in mind when I signed on to do this program.

241

Event: Acropolis
Series: World Championship
Headquarters: Lagonissi, Greece
Date: May 28-31, 1984
Length: 2,258 km. (stages: 47—797 km.)
Co-driver: Fred Gallagher
Result: Fifth Overall

## Athens, Greece (June 1, AP)

Sweden's Stig Blomqvist with co-driver Bjorn Cederberg in an Audi Quattro on Thursday won the 2258 kilometer Acropolis Rally, ELPA, Greek organizers of the rally said. Blomqvist's teammate, Hannu Mikkola, was second in an identical Quattro while the best that Lancia could do were third and fourth by Markku Alen (Finland) and Attiligo Bettega (Italy). Two works Peugeots, two works Audis, and two works Lancias fell by the wayside in what many call the roughest event in the World Championship. Best private entry was American John Buffum in his BFGoodrich Audi Quattro.

JB: This was the event of the co-driver. Irishman Fred Gallagher used to be an optician, but he gave that up to become a professional co-driver. He works a lot for Toyota, but at this event he was with me. We spent three days making notes with Terry Harryman, who co-drives for Peugeot's number-one driver, Ari Vatanen. I was pleasantly surprised to find out how similar my notes were to Vatanen's; after all, he is a former World Champion and may well be again in 1985.

The practice Quattro broke down twice, and we ended up doing most of our notes in a rental car. There were times when I thought that my pair of world-class co-drivers had us lost. At one point, I was convinced that Fred had us running down a dry creek bed. It turned out to be the stage. Practice is not much fun. In fact, practice sucks, but it does have its moments.

242

*21-1 1984 Acropolis World Championship Rally
(Greece): JB, Fred Gallagher and Audi Quattro on
stage below Kalambaka Monestary.*

Sitting in the *agora* or market place of the tiny village
of Distomona on a spring afternoon having a wonderful
ice cream, helped me realize just how lucky we are. It is
great to have a profession that allows us to travel all over
the world and see and do things that many people only get
to read about. I really appreciate it very much.

This was a co-driver's event because we drove to a
pace, and Fred helped me keep that pace. He kept
reminding me that we could let the hot dogs destroy

themselves and move up as they fell out. That's what happened. We were tenth after the first day, eighth after the second day and fifth at the finish. It was the best finish ever by an American at a major world championship event, and we were very happy with it. But it was not as though we drove to the limit and beat a bunch of people. We drove our event and let the chips fall.

The Acropolis is the event where the BFGoodrich program really began getting attention. We were running on regular street tires, none of those rally specials for us. BFG is committed to competing on its production tires, and that's just fine with me. The Acropolis is supposed to be as tough as rallies get. We had a total of two punctures in 1400 miles of rally, almost all of it on gravel. Everyone else—and I mean everyone else—destroyed tires by the truckload. I heard that the Lancia team had sixteen punctures the first day.

We did not even practice or make notes on the final long leg of the rally, which is a night section on the Peloponnesian Peninsula. We borrowed Vatanen's notes from Harryman and found them to be excellent substitutes for our own.

The awards were presented on the Philopappos Hill with the Acropolis in the background. Maybe it was there that I decided that rallying wasn't such a bad way to make a living after all.

Event: Hunsruck
Series: European Championship
Headquarters: Trier, Germany
Date: August 16-19, 1984
Length: 1,035 km. (stages: 26 - 450 km.)
Co-driver: Neil Wilson
Result: Fourth overall

## Trier, West Germany
## (August 19, Trierischer Volksfreund)

German Champion Harald Demuth won the Hunsrick rally by nearly two minutes from a pair of fellow country-men. Demuth's Audi Quattro was too much for the Opel Manta 400 of Erwin Weber and the Porsche Turbo of Manfred Hero, who overcame several mechanical problems to climb into third in the late going. Group A honors went to Englishman Tony Pond in an Austin Rover Vitesse. American John Buffum fell off the pace in the late going, finally dropping to fourth in his BFGoodrich Audi Quattro.

JB: Some rallies are fun, some aren't. This one wasn't. I cut my teeth rallying in Germany when I was in the army, playing lieutenant in my Porsche. The first European championship event I ever won was in Germany, so I have some very good memories of rallying in Germany. But the stages at the Hunsruck rally are sort of artificial. Many of them are on the U.S. military base at Baumholder and consist of straights connected by ninety-degree corners. The rally had a lot more tarmac than I remembered from earlier years, so that most of the top cars were running slicks for the whole event. We went with Comp T/As, which were fine as a compromise but couldn't match the speed of the slicks on asphalt.

Practice here is unique because it is not free. The organizers schedule it for a certain time and you practice and make your notes then or not at all. You get two passes at the road and that's it. We did the practice in an Audi 80 (4000) Quattro that I borrowed from the Audi works in Ingolstadt. We also managed to sneak in some after-hours practice in a borrowed Mercedes.

We started okay, but the car was not running right. It seemed to have a problem getting enough fuel. The crew changed fuel pumps six times without any effect. I think the fuel cell was plumbed wrong or something. Anyway, it ran poorly and there were a few times when I wondered if the engine was going to start. Then halfway through the last day, the transmission began making loud, nasty-sounding noises. I think the crown wheel and pinion were wearing. We decided to let up and take the pressure off it. That allowed Hero to pass us. We could have beaten him, especially after he had clutch trouble, if our car had been healthy. We might have even been able to take Weber, too. But Demuth, in what amounts to a factory Quattro on his home turf, no way.

When I returned the car to Audi, I had a chance to see a lot of people, including Audi Sport boss Roland Gumpert. We were able to make arrangements to get an A-2 manifold, an electric clutch, a close-ratio transmission and a bunch of other stuff. I had decided that if we were going to do well, the car needed to be updated to A-2 specs. I took the parts to Sutton in England so they could get it done before Cyprus.

Event: Cyprus Rally
Series: European Championship
Headquarters: Nicosia, Cyprus
Date: September 28-30, 1984
Length: 1,261 km. (stages: 38—661 km.)
Co-driver: Fred Gallagher
Result: First overall

## Nicosia, Cyprus (September 30, UPI)

John Buffum, the American rally champion, captured the Cyprus rally today in an Audi Quattro for his first major European victory. He and his co-driver Fred Gallagher of Britain clocked 709.31 hours (sic) over a three day, eight-hundred-mile course that included mountain roads and treacherous dirt tracks. Seventy cars from twelve countries started, but only thirty finished.

JB: You know that TV beer commercial where they say, "It doesn't get any better than this?" Sitting here on the pool deck of the Ledra Hotel in Nicosia, I know exactly what they are talking about. We all just took turns throwing one another into the pool—except for David Sutton. The mechanics all have this fantasy about doing it, but they also know who signs the checks.

When we got here two weeks ago, I was hoping down deep that we could win. But when Fred and I went out and started making notes, I began having my doubts. The roads are unbelievably narrow and twisty. In fact, our average winning speed for the rally was less than 35 mph. Fred and I really earned this one. We spent a full week getting notes and practicing the roads and still didn't have time to do all the stages twice. Jerry Rinaldo from BFG said that it takes forever to get anywhere on this island. Jerry had been responsible for getting our tires to the events all season, and no matter where we were—in Greece, Germany, Sardinia—Jerry was there, checking the tires and making sure everything worked.

Since Hunsruck, the Sutton people had installed the short-ratio gearbox, the new injection system and exhaust manifold. They also fitted the electric clutch. A simple button on the gearshift lever allows me to downshift and left-foot brake at the same time. It was super important at this event because of the tight corners (corners within corners, someone said). The new clutch lets me brake, shift and still keep the revs up—to come out of the corner on the boost.

We led from the very first stage, and I was surprised that we could do it so easily. I worked hard, but we weren't taking any chances. On the third stage, we spun and killed the engine and still had the best time on the stage. The competition was excellent and included Carlo Capone in the Lancia, Jimmy McRae in a 240 RS Datsun, Russell Brookes in an Opel Manta 400, and Ilia Tchoubrikov in a Renault 5 Turbo plus several Datsuns and Opels for B-graded drivers we had never heard of.

This is a very long rally with lots of mountains. By the time we got to Paphos on the west coast of the island, we had opened up a 4½-minute lead and I felt quite good about that. On the run back to Nicosia, we were able to pull out even further. We holed the radiator just before the end of the second day, and I got real concerned about temperature. It was okay though, and the crew changed the radiator, welded up the exhaust, replaced the starter and that sort of thing before the *parc ferme* in Nicosia.

The last day was sort of anti-climactic because Capone blew an engine and McRae crashed and we were about ten minutes ahead of Brookes. I let up quite a bit, and was glad I did. Just before the end we met a truck going the other way on a stage! It was no problem, but had we been running 10/10ths, it could have been a disaster.

The hardest part of the last day was the drive back to Nicosia. We were following the BFGoodrich service barge through the crowds. Rinaldo kept throwing BFG stickers and postcards out the window and people would run right in front of us to get a souvenir. We had to keep dodging bodies.

It's odd, I thought I would be more excited about winning. It just sort of seems mundane or something. I wish I could put it into words better. It felt fine, let's say— but not great.

Before the awards ceremony, I threw David Sutton into the pool. Now it feels great!

248

Event: Lombard RAC
Series: World Championship
Headquarters: Chester, England
Date: November 25-29, 1984
Length: 3,231 km. (stages: 56—890 km.)
Co-driver: Neil Wilson
Result: DNF—crash, Stage Forty

## Chester, Cheshire
## (November 30, RAC Press Release)

Ari Vatanen returned to Chester Castle this after-noon as winner of the 1984 Lombard RAC Rally. It was the end of five days and 2,003 miles of hectic competition, during which he survived one incident on Wednesday night when his Peugeot 205 Turbo landed on its roof in a Welsh forest stage. The thirty-two-year-old Finn, with co-driver Terry Harryman from Bangor, NI, returned victorious just forty-one seconds ahead of fellow countryman, Hannu Mikkola, driving an Audi Quattro. It was the smallest winning margin on the Lombard RAC Rally since the event became a round of the World Rally Championship in 1973.

JB: The best of times and the worst of times. This is my favorite rally in the entire world. I have run it seven times and in 1983 finished sixth. Because it is not a practice event, it is much more like U.S. rallies. I have a lot of good friends here, so it is almost like a home event. In my opinion, it is the most important rally in the World Championship: the level of competition is always unbe-lievably high—something like ten A-priority drivers and twenty B-types.

I usually beat the hell out of the car, sometimes try too hard, always go off the road in the Kielder Forest in

249

Scotland, and have earned a reputation in the British press of driving in the ditches. On this event I have rolled, crashed, and broken on the last stage. In 1984 I feel like I moved half a step closer to being in a very exclusive club of drivers.

For four days we ran third behind two former World Champions in works 4WD cars. On several stages, we beat them outright—so badly in one case that the organizers did not believe our time and added a minute just to make it look better. (They later removed the minute.)

This was one of the all-time highs that I have ever experienced in racing. Everything was going for us. The car worked very well. The BFG street tires were perfect (so perfect that on the last night of the rally, Hannu Mikkola tried to get some for himself). The conditions were just what we wanted: rain and mud. There were only about eight hours of daylight each day, making me very happy that I had re-signed with Hella lights. Neil was doing a great job of reading the maps. It was fantastic.

That made our accident on the fortieth stage even more of a downer. We had been running in the top three for several stages and in retrospect, should have slowed down just a bit. In the fog and dark it is very hard to judge your pace. You always feel like everyone is going faster.

It was only about a thirty-degree right-hander, but when I saw it, I knew we were too fast—maybe 100-plus mph. I tried to tuck inside to save it, but there was a footpath coming in from the right and it made a bump in the road. The bump caused the suspension to unload and we lost traction. We must have slid sixty or eighty feet into a bog. Even with the 4WD, we couldn't get out. If there had been twenty spectators, we could have got going again. As it was, we ended up walking 1½ miles to the finish control. When we recovered the car it didn't have a scratch on it.

250

At 11:00 P.M. on Wednesday, November 28, just outside Resolven, Wales, our 1984 European rally season came to an end."

**JB** "Looking back, there are some things that stick in my memory about my season in Europe. I remember the time Neil Wilson and I trashed a rental car while practicing in Sardinia. We came over a little knoll and there was another car, backing up to check a pacenote. I tried to stuff us past on his right side and hit a wall. So we had to get another rental car.

The rental companies knew about the rally and knew a lot of teams were using their cars for practice and pacenoting, so we had to camouflage ourselves.

We bought a very nice polo tennis shirt for Neil and sent him in to rent a car. He was an English journalist checking out a land purchase. Of course he pulled it off beautifully.

Luckily we only had one day of practice left because we were scared shitless. The rental car had no seat belts. Practicing is probably more dangerous than running the actual rally—and we had no seat belts.

I also remember our practice sessions for Cyrpus. Each day was a long hard day and Fred Gallagher and I would get to the hotel about 8:00 P.M. each night. Then we'd rush around cleaning up and go over to this little open-air restaurant. Lovely place. Seventy degrees each night.

So one night, when Fred and the mechanic are ready to go back to the hotel, I decide to join some locals and drink a little wine. Fred said, 'No, you don't want to do that. And of course I said, 'Sure, I do want to do that.'

Mistake. The next day was no picnic. I could just barely fit my head inside the practice car. Fred was very good to me that day. He had us stop about 4:00 P.M. and I sat by the pool and recuperated.

Two days later Fred and I again went out to eat and had a couple bottles of good wine and the next day he's sicker than hell. Everytime we'd come to the start of a stage he'd get out, lean on a eucalyptus tree and throw up. Just to show him what a really nice guy I was, I'd back up a couple of hundred yards each time to allow him to be sick in private. I'm really a good guy.

In Sardinia, on the Costa Smeralda Rally, between my first and second accident, a Ferrari 308 tied me for fastest time on a mountain stage. I thought a Ferrari was a strange car to use on a professional rally, but I thought it even stranger that a Ferrari and an Audi Quattro could equal each other's times on a mountain road.

A nice thing happened after our fifth place finish on the Acropolis in Greece. There was a lot of Audi brass at the awards presentation because a Quattro had won the rally. Dr. Ferdinand Piech, the head of Audi, and Roland Gumpert, the man in charge of Audi Sport, were both there and Dr. Piech took his own Audi Sport lightweight jacket off and gave it to me to wear when I received my trophy. I thought that was a very nice gesture.

During our practice sessions on Cyprus I got a bit drunk one night at a bar on the west end of the island. Days later, during the rally, we passed that same bar and there was a crowd out front waving at us and jumping up and down. We waved back as we passed by.

The rally car arrived on Cyprus after we had finished our pacenotes so Fred Gallagher and I decided to try it on a few roads. There wasn't any rule against us running stage roads so we ran one that Fred had some past records for—but he didn't tell me. There wasn't much traffic, but I drove 80 percent when I couldn't see and 90 percent when I could.

At the end of the stage we were sitting in a little village and Fred said he thought it had gone pretty well—but he kept smiling. When I asked him what he was smiling about he told me I had beaten Jimmy McRae's fastest time from the year before by five seconds. McRae had won the rally the year before.

For the first time I began to believe I could finally win a major European rally during that year.

Cyprus was a good win for me because I beat Jimmy McRae and Carlo Capone, who went on to become the European rally champion that same year, driving for Lancia.

The RAC is my favorite rally in the entire world—back when it was a secret rally. Now, with pacenotes, it sucks.

In '84 I set fastest time on about 10 percent of the stages and won five forest stages outright. The organizers didn't believe my time on one stage and added a full minute to our score, but Neil had them check their logs and they reversed themselves and removed the extra minute.

Sutton Park is one of the opening day paved spectator stages that always draws a huge number of spectators. The '84 RAC was a secret rally but *Motoring News* printed a map for spectators the week before the start.

Since I didn't have much to do because there was no pacenoting allowed, I took a rental car and drove Sutton Park by myself. I just drove around leisurely looking for a place to have lunch. At one point I was blocked by a locked gate and had to drive around and come back from the other side to finish the stage. That gate was at the end of a long uphill blind crest where you could really make some time . . . if you knew it went straight over the crest. Otherwise you'd have to slow down a bit.

I'd never done well on Sutton Park because I used BFG Comp T/As on wet asphalt while everyone else used racing tires. But that year I won the Sutton Park Stage.

I told the organizers I'd driven the road some days before the rally started but they didn't want to hear about it. They didn't want to know.

I suppose I was guilty of judiciously circumventing the rules but in the end it didn't matter.

And finally I'll never forget the day Neil Wilson and I pulled over while practicing in Sardinia. We just sat in the car and looked over the countryside, thinking how lucky we were to be in that place at that time; getting to see different parts of the world; having fun doing something we loved—something challenging and interesting . . . and doing it all on someone else's buck.

We had so many interesting good times and we were so fortunate to have the ability, or just the good luck, to be sent to all those places, to do a job and at the same time see Sardinia, Germany, Greece, the Ivory Coast, Cyprus, Portugal, England—and of course, rallying takes you to places most tourists never visit, which is just another bonus.

It was great when we were practicing overseas and we'd come through a small town or village and stop at some little place for an ice cream. We'd stand out there in the middle of nowhere, surrounded by people who didn't speak our language, and over there, the people know all about rallying. We were a major attraction. Lots of hero worship, autographs—great for the ego. 'A rally driver! Wow!'

It's a great feeling inside. Excitement and interest wherever we went. Very few teams ever experience that feeling in our own country. We were very fortunate!"

# PART FIVE

JB                    (Photo: Thomas Barker)

# 22

# In Retrospect
## Handing Off

**W**HEN JOHN BUFFUM retired from full-time competition at the close of his perfect season in 1987 he did not abandon the sport that had become his life—professional rallying. Instead, he decided to contribute, to give something back to the game, to use his reputation and experience to make it better.

He accepted a position with the Sports Car Club of America as National PRO Rally Steward, and ultimately, the series national manager.

In addition, he increased support of his stepson's rally career. With the benefit of JB's experience and encouragement, and a lot of hard work, Paul ("Thumper") Choiniere, took the SCCA/CASC North American Rally Cup in 1988, 1989 and 1992—and in 1990 Paul became the SCCA National PRO Rally Driving Champion. He repeated that feat in 1992. The family tradition continues.

Today John stays active with several activities both inside and outside the sport. His Libra International Racing shop builds and maintains rally cars for several teams; he referees high school hockey games; and he and his wife, Mary, care for several foster children in their Vermont home.

And every once in a while he dusts off his helmet, packs his driving suit, and once again enjoys his sport from the perspective from which it all started . . . as a driver.

The following are some reflections and opinions of North America's master of professional rallying:

## On the past, present and future of the sport:

"Looking back I think I came into rallying at just about the right time, at the beginning of the seventies. In '73, when the national championship series began, rallying was a very small and unknown closet sport in the U.S. and Canada. It was just beginning and wasn't much of anything—just a 'private' sport.

Then David Ash stepped forth with NARA and pulled in Pirelli, Volkswagen, Lancia, Triumph, Porsche+Audi, and The Montgomery Ward Auto Club, and the sport began to grow and continued to grow until 1980 because of the competition between the two national sanctioning groups.

Professional rallying took another half to full step upward in the U.S. from 1982 through 1984 when BFGoodrich became involved and when European rallying also enjoyed a period of substantial growth. We took another step up when PRO rally cars were included as a separate class in the Pikes Peak Auto Hill Climb where they eventually established several new records in that famous event.

Then, in 1986 we took a step backwards and finally leveled off in '88 and '89, returning to the level we experienced during the '75-'80 era. We finally realized professional rallying would never be a major sport in North America and we all decided to build a sport for ourselves—the organizers, sponsors, competitors, officials, supporters—everyone who was personally involved.

Today there is still some manufacturer involvement, still some interest out there. Subaru sponsors the national championship series. The public knows more about us than it did fifteen years ago, but despite that increased awareness the amount of media attention is down quite a bit because it is no longer a new sport, and because we promised the moon for several years, and did not deliver.

Because of decreased media coverage, reaching new segments of the public has become far more difficult.

I believe the reason media coverage has fallen off is that we are not providing anything new. It's the same story over and over.

People have often asked me during the past ten years, 'Why hasn't professional rallying gotten bigger in the U.S. as it has in most other countries?'

Well, I personally don't think it will ever be as big as it is in Europe. It just doesn't warrant the interest enjoyed by other major spectator sports in this country. It doesn't mean that it is still a 'closet' sport, it just means it will never be a 'major' sport in the U.S.

First, the country is too large. It's too spread out. Western Europe is about half the size of the U.S. and everybody is much closer together—several countries, each with their individual national interests, in a relatively small area.

Second, Europeans are brought up to enjoy their cars. For instance, we drive to get from Point A to Point B on a freeway system that is very good. For Europeans, part of the reason for going from A to B is the fun they have driving their cars. With us, it's getting there that counts. In Europe it's the fun of getting there that counts.

Thirdly, our entire television sports coverage is just great. But there's so much of it that it's tough to break in with something new. Because of the distances that must be traveled to go stand in the woods and watch a professional rally, most Americans would prefer to stay home, become couch potatoes, and watch baseball, football, hockey, golf, basketball, boxing, tennis, auto racing—even thumb wrestling from Las Vegas. And most of those sports can be seen at the same time by just using the remote control to switch channels.

259

Also, because of the nature of the sport, with its courses stretching hundreds of miles, it is very difficult to film. Television crews cannot set up a few strategically placed stationary cameras and catch all the action. They have to constantly be on the move to keep up with a rally. Very costly.

In 1983-86 professional rallying was often seen on TV. ESPN featured most of the World Championship Rally Series. And back then more manufacturers were involved in North America, with a lot more bucks than today. Audi, Mazda, Peugeot, Dodge, Toyota, Subaru and several others sponsored teams in our national championship series.

Then, of course, BFGoodrich stepped in. They had the largest manufacturer involvement in rallying for several years and were the prime sponsor of television coverage which brought the sport to more of the public.

BFG spent their money wisely and well. Audi and Mazda spent their budgets running sponsored teams in their cars. BFG did not sponsor a particular car or team. They spent their money on publicity. Audi would spend $100,000 to support a single car, but BFG spent the same $100,000 to publicize the sport, which is why I say BFG had the biggest impact on the sport in our country.

The combination was perfect. The auto manufacturers put out the product and BFGoodrich publicized it.

Then in '84 they gave me the financing to do rallies in Europe, supported ESPN with advertising dollars, and suddenly rallying got a lot more television coverage in the U.S. When I went to Europe I ran BFG 'American' street tires, and that increased the level of domestic interest and the sport benefited, and continued to grow.

Bridgestone then replaced BFG as the prime sponsor of the SCCA PRO Rally National Championships but they were not prepared to spend the same level of dollars that had been provided by BFG. Bridgestone's entire budget commitment (we were told it was $50,000) was spent within the rally community. But BFG did not spend their money inside the rally community. They didn't give SCCA a lot of money to buy the series. They put their money in the right place—national publicity. They brought rallying to the media. They brought Rod Millen and me before the viewing public. They printed posters and programs and finally sent an American driver to Europe.

I also think David Ash's 'star system' concept was very good for the sport. It gave the public someone to identify with: a Richard Petty, an Arnold Palmer, a Jimmy Connors, a Muhammad Ali—someone who immediately established the vision of, and increased personal interest in a particular sport.

Today we no longer have a star system.

When I retired in 1987 and Rod Millen left the sport in this country two years later, there just wasn't anyone ready to step up and take our place as the new 'star' of professional rallying.

It's like the horse and the cart. Today we don't have a real star because we don't have the attractive money involvement and the series does not have substantial money involvement because there is no star grabbing the public's interest, and in turn, the advertiser's and sponsor's interest–and money.

Today we are waiting for one driver to emerge from the pack. We're waiting for our Jack Nicklaus to replace our Arnold Palmer. We need someone who is a very good driver with a very good dominant car, who wins most of the important rallies and has a good personality and the charisma to grab the public's interest. But even then, it would take $100,000 or so to publicize him or her for professional rallying to benefit in the U.S.

I personally doubt that it will happen.

In 1988, the first year I became the SCCA PRO rally steward, we faced a major insurance crisis just as many other businesses at that time. In a country where everyone was suing everyone else over just about anything at all, auto racing was looked upon as very risky business by insurance carriers. And of course PRO rallyists were a very small segment of SCCA and many of their directors felt that because of the nature of our sport—racing on public roads with spectators standing nearby— we could subject them to major financial exposure.

Virginia Reese was about to exit her position as chairperson of the SCCA PRO Rally board and together we met with the board of directors and reviewed our safety programs and

*22.1 The tradition continues: John Buffum and Paul Choiniere, Jr.*

future plans and got us past that problem.

I think the SCCA board of directors felt comfortable with me, a well known and trusted person with good name recognition, taking over management of the sport. This helped solve our insurance problem and allowed us to start slowly rebuilding the sport.

Since then professional rallying has experienced slow but steady growth, primarily designed for enjoyment of the participants and a fair return for manufacturers on their advertising dollars.**"**

## On learning to be a rally driver:

**"**There are two ways to learn how to be a rally driver. You can go for broke all the time—like I did when I started. You wreck a few cars, have a few crashes . . . but it's the fastest way to learn, if you survive physically and financially.

Or you can start slowly and learn as you go. The more you learn the faster you'll drive, building up slowly.

I was self-taught in competitive rally driving, just as I was in golf, tennis and skiing. It was only about 1984 or '85 before I learned to look way down the road and not right in front of the car. I never knew it while I was driving for Triumph, but the Quattro was so fast I had to learn to look forward to be able to anticipate things so much more quickly—because they happened so much more quickly.

I also learned to look at the trees on the outside of a corner, as far around it as I could see—that's how you judge the severity of a corner. That's when experience counts so much.

Reading the road in front of you is far more important than knowing how to drive the car well. The guy reading the road is going to do a better job of maintaining his speed. I also learned that from experience—miles under the wheels.

A good driver categorizes corners. As you come into a corner you categorize it. You make decisions so quickly because your mind works just like a computer. You see something that reminds you that you've seen that same type of corner before, perhaps years before . . . maybe the same tree line or something else. That's experience.

If you've seen 10,000 corners you can categorize them into one hundred and you'll see ten of each kind on a rally. But if you've only seen one hundred corners . . . .

It's like drawing a graphed curve. You'll draw a better curve having more experience factors . . . more reference dots on the graph to connect. The more points you can plot on the graph, the more perfect your drawn curve will be.

When I started I had the coordination and the ability to drive fast but I had very few experience dots on my graph. Today I have hundreds of dots to get me through the perfect curve at a much higher speed without consciously thinking about it.

I was fortunate to be born with very good coordination. I can do a lot of different physical things very well. Experience just made me better.

Of course experience also teaches you what to do when you're just going much too fast, despite all that information available to you. That's when experience will save you— perhaps save your life.**

## On mountain driving, night driving, and cornering:

**I remember driving in southern France with Vicki in 1968 or thereabouts. I don't know if we were practicing for a rally or just driving somewhere, doing something else. But I do remember driving along this road in the Alps and being scared shitless.

I slowed right down. We were up in the mountains and there was nothing down on the right side and a rock face on the left. I remember thinking to myself, 'I'm scared.' I drove along at 30 mph just to get down to the bottom.

But in rallying I don't drive much differently in the mountains than on the flat. I can hang the front wheel out in space, providing it's on the inside of a corner. I really think about it only when I'm passing someone. I realize I'm up high on the edge of a cliff, like the Spyder Lake Stage on the Olympus in Washington, but it doesn't affect my driving style.

In daylight you can see so much more. You can see the zigzag of a road; you can look through the trees and see where the road comes out. At night, even with the very brightest driving lights, you still cannot see all that.

I think it requires more experience and skill to drive well at night because of the limited line of sight. You try to take more things into consideration at night because they seem to come at you so much quicker. You have to 'sense' the surroundings because you can't 'see' as far down the road and because your peripheral vision does not work as well at night as it does in daylight.

Today I think our U.S. rally drivers are not as good at night as we used to be because we have far more daylight stages today than we used to have. In the old days all the stages were at night. We got a lot more night experience than the young driver gets today.

I think that's one of the reasons I did well on the RAC rallies in England. Most European rallies are run during daylight hours, but the RACs run in November and three quarters of the stages were always at night.

Of course I also did well on the RACs because they were secret rallies—the only world championship event that did not allow pacenotes until very recently. And all our North American championship rallies were secret—no pacenotes. So, by removing the great advantage of pacenotes from the top European drivers who grew up on them and used them at almost every rally, it made a much more level playing field and I got a lot closer to them.

It doesn't matter to me if a curve goes right or left, although I prefer to be on the inside because I have more precise knowledge of where the exact inside of the corner is, or the exact edge of the corner. If it's on my side I can point right at the trees and know exactly where I am. In a right-hand corner, towards the co-driver's side, I have to keep more power in hand because I'm not so certain where the exact corner or edge is because its six feet away from me and I can't see it as clearly.

I may hang a wheel off on the co-driver's side on a right-hander, only because I can't tell exactly where it is. Co-drivers always feel a driver will cut a corner much tighter if it's on their side and not on the driver's side, especially in the mountains. But that's not really so—the driver just can't pinpoint the edge of the road as well on the co-driver's side.

I mean, we're both going to the same place aren't we?"

## On four-wheel-drive vs. two-wheel-drive:

"The four-wheel-drive Quattro was so much better than the two-wheel-drive cars everybody else drove that at first I didn't need to be that good to win—the car was that much better.

To begin with, when I moved into a 4WD car I could not drive it nearly as well as I could the 2WD Triumph. It was especially evident in my first rally with the Quattro—the Nor'wester Rally in Washington. Rod Millen would have beaten me but he got blocked by another car (Guy Light) and had some sort of engine problem—vapor-lock or something—that shut him down on a stage for a minute and a half. I only beat him by a half-minute.

I had the experience, I had the ability, I had the better car, and yet I was getting beat.

After that rally I realized what was happening. It was because I was applying front-wheel-drive techniques to a four-

266

wheel-drive car. With front-wheel-drive you control the attitude of the car with the brake. With rear-wheel-drive you control the attitude with the throttle. With four-wheel-drive you balance between the brake and throttle to keep the car in an attitude so you can use the advantages of 4WD to accelerate as soon as possible out of a corner. You use the advantages of power and improved 4WD traction to accelerate out of the corner and down the straight-away.

After I figured out what I was doing I was much better the next rally and kept improving until I stopped in 1987.

Thinking back on my Quattro experience brings another point to mind: to be a very good rally driver requires experience, an ability to read the road, the coordination to handle the car, the physical fitness required in professional rallying—and perhaps most important—the intelligence to quickly put all these factors together at the same time.

If you have a slow computer and you feed all this data into it, you will crash before you get an answer. Your computer needs to be up to speed—you have to have the intelligence to quickly make use of all the constantly changing data."

## On Rallying in Europe vs. North America:

"Professional rallies in North America are sprint races. Stages are fairly short and compact compared to those overseas and total stage miles on our events are about 120 miles. In North America you can lose an entire rally because of a single flat tire. There is not enough time to make up a couple of lost minutes, so we go along at a more careful pace. We have to take care of the car so we don't lose time breaking things—time that we cannot recover on our short courses.

We probably drive nine-tenths on a North American championship rally.

But in Europe you have to push the car to the limit, or very close to it, because the competition is so much more fierce.

You need to drive much harder and much faster than over here. You have to raise the level of your performance to compete overseas and you have to demand much more from the car.

Therefore, a lot more service time is required overseas because the cars are pushed so much harder. That's one of the main differences between a privateer and a factory driver, both in our country and overseas—a fact I don't think many people realize.

A factory driver can push to the outer limits, knowing he has service capabilities available to keep the equipment running. A privateer has to pamper the equipment a bit because he doesn't have equal service capabilities.

When I went overseas with the Triumphs and Audis we often used pickup service crews. Then, when the cars began to fall apart I'd have to slow down. If I kept trying I'd just compound the problems and have to go even slower in the long run.

It's very difficult for a driver to resist driving at the same level as his competition. So when I went over there I wanted to compete, to drive hard all the time, and that increased my chances of going off or damaging the car.

That's probably why I went off more overseas than I did here in North America because I was always trying that extra tenth to show what I could do against the very best in the world. I wasn't driving eleven-tenths but that extra tenth or half a tenth was more than I usually drove in our national championship series. So of course the problems were increased by that extra bit.

I always thought it would have been interesting to see what I would have done overseas with real rally tires, rather than with BFGoodrich street tires. Although BFG was very good to me and I couldn't have done many of the European rallies without them, people would often ask me what I was doing with those zilch tires.

Real rally tires would have made a big difference in my performance in Europe. On my final RAC Rally the BFGs were very good because it was warm and wet, and for the most part they were excellent on the Acropolis, because it was rough and loose surfaced. However, tires would have made a big difference on the Costa Smeralda or the Hunsruck Rally, but of course I did well anyway—because of a clearly superior car and the fact that I was driving very well.

The combination couldn't be beat and we worked very hard on those rallies. Harder than most anyone else.

I guess you can summarize the differences between North American rallying and European rallying by comparing triple A baseball to the big leagues—Europe is the big leagues.**"**

## On dealing with the public and other competitors:

**"**I have often heard that I am stand-offish and egotistical; that I don't communicate well with people because I just don't want to.

I don't honestly see myself that way at all. To begin with I'm from Vermont and Vermonters are sort of different. They are very independent, even more so than Texans. They are often more outspoken and will not try to smooth it over when they tell you to go screw yourself.

The fact that I often don't talk to people is not because i am conceited. It's just that I am not a naturally gregarious person; I don't feel comfortable talking to strangers. On the other hand, once I know someone, have time, and am talking about a subject I know and enjoy, it is sometimes very hard to shut me up.

I think my reluctance to talk to strangers is only a fault if you believe that John Buffum should talk to everybody because he is a champion.**"**

269

## On comparisons of other North American rally drivers:

"Jean Paul Perusse and I talked in 1978 about the relative merits of our driving and how we would do in world class rallying. I was always guarded or pessimistic, you might say. Jean Paul said we'd do well overseas. He felt that without pacenotes we'd do quite well. As the years passed by I realized he was right. I think I proved that in '83 and '84 when I went to Europe.

Jean Paul was a very good driver. He and I and Taisto Heinonen had some good battles many years ago. When I first started in the late '70s I did not know if I could beat Jean Paul. That was the way I felt back then. In the U.S. there was Hendrik Blok, Eric Jones, Scott Harvey and Gene Henderson . . . yes, I could beat them. I was faster than they were but at first I thought I had to keep going all the time—had to drive ten-tenths all the time—and I'd crash.

But it wasn't the same in Canada. Jean Paul was just barely ahead of me. I could beat him sometimes but at first I felt I was the underdog. However, by 1977 he rarely ever beat me.

Then there was Taisto and Walter Boyce (who never fulfilled his potential). Taisto was very good, may have been better than Jean Paul, but he was from Western Canada and we didn't compete in the same events very often. I also felt he lacked the competitive drive. Walter, on the other hand, had his heyday before 1975 when I really got going and after that he never seriously challenged us again.

During the four years I drove a Triumph, Taisto won the Canadian national championship in a Toyota Celica. If you check results in Europe back then you'd find that the Toyota and Triumph were fairly even cars. Yet, results in North American rallying would show that I beat the Canadian drivers more times than they beat me.

I think it was then I finally began to believe I was a pretty damn good rally driver.

Obviously the most frequent comparisons were made between Rod Millen and me. Roddy started rallying in New Zealand in the early '70s, and according to the results I've seen, he was their national champion when he came to the U.S. in 1977. He brought his sponsors (Mazda) with him and they were instantly the major competition for me.

Millen was a professional from the word 'GO' and had as much experience as I did in 1977. However, starting in 1977 I began rallying in Europe where the competition was very intense.

By European standards I was grossly under-sponsored and my limited successful results throughout the 1977-1983 period highlighted that fact.

But what did happen was that I progressed faster to a much higher degree of proficiency than Rodney. By constantly being driven to go faster to 'keep up' in Europe, my nine-tenths became the equal of Millen's ten-tenths.

Millen was, and still is, an excellent driver, be it rallying or off-road racing, and his Mazda RX-7 4WD was an excellent car, almost the equal of the original Audi Quattro A1. He obviously had the required coordination and physical attributes since he'd won some tough rallies around the world. So what was the difference? Why did I beat him so consistently?

It wasn't because I feared losing. I never thought about that. It wasn't an overwhelming desire to win no matter what the cost.

Perhaps I had that extra 'something' that's so hard to define in competition; perhaps it was because Millen drove the same no matter what the circumstances—like the year he had the national championship won on the final rally in Nevada and continued driving the same speed until he crashed and lost it all;

22.2 Rod Millen: Mazda
RX-7

22.3 Jon Woodner: Peugeot
20T-16

22.4 Taisto Heinonen: Toyota
Corolla

22.5 Hendrik Blok: Mazda GLC

22.6 Walter Boyce: Toyota Corolla

(All Photos: Su Kemper)

*22.7 John Woolf: Mazda RX-3*

*22.8 Gene Henderson: Jeep Wagoneer*

*22.9 Dick Turner: I-H Scout*

*22.10 Scott Harvey: Dodge Aspen*

*22.11 Jim Walker: Volvo*

*(All Photos: Su Kemper)*

perhaps he was not able to put things into proper perspective as well as I. Or, perhaps it was a combination of all three things. I don't know."

## On Co-drivers:

"Having a co-driver (navigator) sitting next to you is one of the great differences between being a race driver and a rally driver. For a rally driver, the co-driver's presence doesn't enter into the equation, unless something happens. I usually never even thought about it.

But put a race driver on a cliff, with a co-driver sitting beside him, and he will worry too much about the safety of his passenger since he's trained to only worry about himself.

Having a co-driver beside me is about the same as having a navigating light. Either it's on or it's off. I always liked it better when the navigating light was on. It's like closing one eye and trying to guess how far away an object is. It's difficult to tell without something to relate to.

For a rally driver it's a very subtle relationship. For a race driver it would be a major distraction.

In the U.S. (without pacenotes) a good co-driver will (or should) just put his (or her) feet against the bracing plate and sit there calmly because a driver will sense a co-driver's tension and that will distract him and break his concentration.

A driver wants a co-driver to be smooth, calm and business-like. A non-entity. The co-driver's job is just to keep the ball in play and let me do my thing with it.

A co-driver's role is not exactly that of a servant but, essentially, that's the role they play. They should calm the driver, make sure he has everything he wants, make sure everything remains smooth. The only tension the driver should feel is that caused by his own driving. He shouldn't have to worry about timing, course following, control workers, route instructions, service, etc.—just driving the car. That is the co-driver's role: to take all that responsibility away from the driver and let him do his own thing . . . driving . . .which is what wins professional rallies.

I remember seeing a video of Ari Vatanen on The Manx Rally; he reached over and patted Terry Harriman's knee and said, 'It's okay.' They were going sideways across a wet cattle guard when he did it. I did that once to Tom Grimshaw, when I realized the situation we were in. We were very high up on a mountain cliff in Washington, going downhill into a tight right-hander and we had one of those long 'quiet' slides when it seems the engine has shut off and the car is just going to keep sliding right off the edge. I knew I had it under control, but I didn't know if Tom knew it and there was enough time to let him know. So I reached over, patted his knee and said, 'I've got it.'

I think he appreciated it because he's mentioned it several times.

Of course I also remember saying, 'I've got it' in Arkansas, on a long slippery down hill left-hander—and we went straight off into the woods.

Today when I see a young driver working with an older, experienced co-driver, I see them doing much better than expected. The young driver's learning curve is much steeper because of the experience and knowledge of his older co-driver.

An experienced co-driver can sense when his driver is losing his concentration, or driving on the edge—going too fast for the level of his ability. At this point the experienced co-driver may be able to slow his driver before disaster strikes and they end their rally off the road. And, because the co-driver is the more experienced of the two, a young driver will more readily accept his suggestions.

. Today an experienced co-driver is a calming influence who will often warn a young driver about bad corners, extra rough road sections and hidden dangers the co-driver has encountered before. In the early days we didn't have experienced 'guides.' We crashed on bad corners and left our names to commemorate the deed: 'Henderson's Stump,' 'Taisto's Bridge,' 'Harvey's Tree,' 'Shepherd's Hairpin,' Buffum's Firebreak,' etc.

An experienced co-driver can also influence a young driver's stage times. Most young drivers have not yet developed full confidence when approaching a corner. They often slow down far too early, hunting and pecking for the execution point of an instruction. An experienced co-driver will soon remove that doubt and the young driver will learn that the corner is always where he is told it will be. He will soon learn to trust his co-driver and not slow down before it is necessary. Maintaining his speed closer to the execution points of several hundred turns during a rally can have a very good affect on a young driver's stage times.

I think that in U.S. professional rallying a winning performance consists of: 40 percent driver, 30 percent car, 10 percent co-driver, 10 percent service crew—and 10 percent luck.

I have a pretty short list of favorite co-drivers: Fred Gallagher, Neil Wilson, Doug Shepherd, and Tom Grimshaw.

Fred is what I call a 'co-driver's co-driver,' the total professional. I remember a stage on the Acropolis Rally in Greece when we were using Ari Vatanen's pacenotes. At one point we were going along and the notes said 'Long flat right— 50 metres,' but as we came around the long flat right there was a fork in the road that wasn't even in Ari's notes. I really didn't know which way to go. Fred, being the pro he is, had the route book open to that correct page, under his pacenotes, and as I slowed a bit he said, 'Oh, stay left.' Now how many co-drivers

276

would have the foresight to read pacenotes constantly and still have the route book open to the correct place to immediately pick up such a problem? I doubt many would be able to do that.

Neil is a professional real estate agent. He's a businessman who enjoys rallying as a second avocation. He was a very good English road rally navigator in the seventies and was very good with maps. He rode with Brian Culcheth in an Opel Manta for many years and won the British Group One Championship in 1977. He also won the 1985 RAC World Championship Rally with Henri Toivonen the year before Henri was killed on the Tour de Corse Rally and has co-driven for Ari Vatanen. So you can see, although he is really just a part-time co-driver and a full-time businessman in England, he's also an excellent and experienced co-driver.

I think Doug was perhaps the quickest study of the four. He picked things up so fast. He was very young when he came with me, but he was also very intelligent and soaked everything up like a sponge. He absorbed everything and really got into it. He was always able to do a lot of work in his head, jump around in the route book, keep track of things spontaneously and instantaneously. When Doug and I ran together I was also fairly young in the sport and we got along very well.

And Tom—well, we ended up together at the perfect time for both of us. We'd been around the sport a long time, had done just about everything, and were ready to have a bit of fun. We'd known each other for years and had struck up a pretty close friendship even before we finally became a team.

Tom worked harder than the others. He wrote notes and instructions out in his route book before we ever started a rally, but then he was involved in the era of the Group B Sport Quattro. The acceleration from Point A to Point B was so much faster than anything we'd experienced before that he didn't have time to think about anything except reading the next instruction. It was a rocket ship and the speed at which things happened was just so fast that I understood why Tom needed to work harder, both before and during rallies.

An indication of the speed and quickness of the Sport Quattro was the fact that I often said, even though I enjoyed co-driving, I would never have co-driven for myself in a Group B Sport Quattro.

But we did have a lot of fun during those final years.**"**

## On being the best of the best:

**"**I don't know when I finally realized that I was good, that I could be the best in North America. I've never had real optimistic feelings. I guess I'm a realist (pessimist?) at heart. I would often think the breaks of the game would end up beating me because I knew the possibility was always there and often I would wait for it to happen.

I think if you said, 'It's going to be a sunny day' and it rained, you'd be devastated. But if you said, 'It's going to rain' and it was sunny, it would be icing on the cake.

I believe, unlike the Wheaties box top which said, 'Champions are made not born,' that you have to be born with some innate qualities to become a champion. You have to have some in-born coordination and perhaps inherited desire. You'll find that very good athletes are good in several sports. There are currently a couple of major league baseball players who are scratch golfers, and there are Bo Jackson and Deion Sanders who play both big league baseball and NFL football. Because of their coordination, they could quickly adapt to other sports.

As a rally driver, you need something a little extra when you move into the high speed events. I'm not sure what that something extra is or how you get it, but I don't think it can be taught. I think you have to be born with that extra percent of talent, effort, determination, and desire that makes a champion. You can work very hard and be very good but without that

278

*22.12 Reserved English businessman, and co-driver, Neil Wilson, checking JB's Audi Quattro into the Wrexham time control on the 1983 RAC World Championship Rally.*

something extra you'll never be great.

There are many drivers out there who have two or three of the traits required to be the best, but perhaps there are not so many who have them all.

I remember Hannu Mikkola telling Tom Grimshaw and me, during a golf game in Washington, that the driver was far more important than the car; that a good driver, to some extent, can overcome a bad car. But a bad driver can never do well in a good car. There were many many times in the final four years when Millen and I would run stages just a few seconds apart until well into a rally. When I ran behind him on the road and had problems with a corner I could see by his tracks that he'd had the same problem at the same spot. That's how close we were as drivers. Then, suddenly, at the end of a stage, Grimshaw would tell me I'd just put a half minute on

279

Roddy. I wouldn't even realize it. Usually I didn't believe him and I'd tell him so. But co-drivers feel things that aren't always obvious to drivers who have to concentrate totally on driving the car, and more times than not, he was right.

Why did that happen time after time? I'm not sure. Perhaps I normally ran along at 90 percent and then, for some unknown reason, I'd try a bit harder and find that extra 10 percent we'd need.

I believe champions think differently. Things become black and white. The longer you are a champion, the more black and white they get. I think a true champion hardly ever competes at 100 percent because his 90 percent is better than most other competitors. But then, when he decides to step up a level, he has that extra click that makes him a champion.

Today, I don't really compete at anything except I think I compete against myself, like on the golf course. I have always competed against myself. I enjoy doing a good job no matter what it is. It satisfies me. I want that self-satisfaction out of whatever I'm doing, whether it be rally driving, golf, tennis or refereeing a hockey game. Perhaps 'compete' is the wrong word. It takes two people to have a competition. Perhaps I just 'strive' for self-satisfaction; for the feeling that I did well, no matter how I did.

The end result may not be so great but I get the personal satisfaction of knowing I did it well.

My wife doesn't understand how I can play golf or tennis and not mind if I get beat. She'll ask what my score was and I'll tell her I don't know; I didn't keep track of it. And she gets upset. She keeps track of everything, like most people."

*22.13 Fred Gallagher (L), John Buffum and David Sutton (R) stand in front of the support crew provided by Sutton for JB's 1984 European adventure. (Photo: Colin Taylor Productions)*

# Epilogue
## Who the Hell is John Buffum?

$T$HE NATIONAL OFFICE OF THE Sports Car Club of America, Inc. is located in Englewood, Colorado. One of the first things a visitor notices upon entering the SCCA building is the framed portraits hanging in the lobby. There are eight of them. They represent the cream of the organization—eight men who are honored for past and present deeds and for contributions to their respective forms of motor sports:

Al Holbert, Scott Pruett, Al Unser, Jr, George Follmer, Paul Newman, Bobby Rahal, Dan Gurney, and American rally driver, John M. Buffum

In 1993 John Buffum left his position as SCCA PRO rally manager to concentrate on his Libra Racing International business and to become more involved in the continuing career of his stepson, Paul.

Libra built two new rally cars at the beginning of the '93 season; an Audi Quattro S2 for Paul and a Ford Escort Cosworth for Carl Merrill, a wealthy resort owner from Maine.

The opening event on the 1993 calendar was the Wild West PRO Rally in the northwest mountain regions of Washington. Paul stayed home that April weekend to be with his wife, who was about to give birth to their third child.

Because of his position as series manager, John Buffum had not driven a national PRO Rally since his retirement in

283

1987. But he no longer held that position and was free to drive Paul's new Audi in Washington.

He was seeded in the number two starting position. And who was seeded number one? Rod Millen, his long time rival and toughest competition during the Audi/Mazda rally wars of the eighties.

Millen had also been absent from the U.S. national circuit for many years. He had concentrated his rally efforts outside the country and had recently won a national championship driving an off-road truck in the Mickey Thompson Stadium Racing series.

Millen was entered in a prototype Hyundai.

Just as in years past, the two most talented professional rally drivers in North America went at it tooth and nail. By the end of the first night Buffum held a thirty-second edge, having won four of the first five stages. But the following day Millen's efforts ended in a DNF when the new Hyundai experienced terminal electrical problems.

John Buffum finished the first 1993 national PRO Rally in the same position he was in at the completion of the 1987 season—in first place, behind the wheel of an Audi Quattro.

And to add icing to the cake, Carl Merrill, driving the Ford Escort Cosworth prepared by Buffum's Libra Racing shop, finished second behind the Quattro.

The six-year vacation had obviously not dulled John Buffum's amazing talents.

In 1988, John Buffum, during his first outing as the SCCA National PRO Rally Steward, was working the opening championship event in Georgia. Late in the evening there was a problem delaying the start of a special stage and JB arrived to straighten it out.

He asked for the control captain and began to give him concise instructions on how to proceed. The control captain interrupted to ask, "Who the hell are you?" John replied, "I'm John Buffum," and continued with his instructions.

Once again the control captain interrupted to ask:

"SO . . . WHO THE HELL IS JOHN BUFFUM?"

*Looking Back (Photo: Martin Holmes)*

# JOHN BUFFUM'S
# NATIONAL CHAMPIONSHIP PROFESSIONAL
# RALLY VICTORIES

| Year/Event | Country | Vehicle | Co-Driver |
|---|---|---|---|
| **1975** | | | |
| Canadian Winter | Canada | Porsche 911 | Vicki |
| 20 Stages | USA | Porsche 911 | Vicki |
| Olympus | USA | Ford Escort | Vicki |
| Happiness Is Sunrise | USA | Ford Escort | Vicki |
| Big Bend Bash | USA | Ford Escort | Vicki |
| Criterium du Quebec | Canada | Porsche 911 | Vicki |
| Sunriser 400 | USA | Ford Escort | Vicki |
| Tall Pines | Canada | Porsche 911 | Vicki |

* SCCA PRO Rally National Champion

| Year/Event | Country | Vehicle | Co-Driver |
|---|---|---|---|
| **1976** | | | |
| Olympus | USA | Porsche 911 | Vicki |
| Northern Lites | USA | Porsche 911 | Vicki |
| Rim of the World | USA | Porsche 911 | Vicki |
| Piston les Wapitis | Canada | Ford Escort | Vicki |
| Lobster Rally | Canada | Ford Escort | Vicki |
| Happiness Is Sunrise | USA | Porsche 911 | Vicki |
| Sunriser 400 | USA | Porsche 911 | Vicki |
| El Diablo | USA | Porsche 911 | Vicki |

* NARA National Rally Champion
* SCCA/CASC North American Rally Cup Champion

| Year/Event | Country | Vehicle | Co-Driver |
|---|---|---|---|
| **1977** | | | |
| Borax Bill Memorial | USA | Porsche 911 | Vicki |
| 100 Acre Wood | USA | Porsche 911 | Vicki |
| Puerto Rico 24-Hours | USA | Porsche 911 | Gene Hauman |
| Piston les Wapitis | Canada | Triumph TR-7 | Vicki |
| La Jornada Trabajosa | USA | Triumph TR-7 | Vicki |
| Highlands Rally | Canada | Triumph TR-7 | Vicki |
| Lobster Rally | Canada | Triumph TR-7 | Vicki |

| Mountain Trials | Canada | Triumph TR-7 | Vicki |
| Rocky Mountain | Canada | Triumph TR-7 | Vicki |
| Ontario Forest Rally | Canada | Triumph TR-7 | Vicki |

* SCCA PRO Rally National Champion
* SCCA/CASC North American Rally Cup Champion

## 1978
| Borax Bill Memorial | USA | Triumph TR-7 | Doug Shepherd |
| 100 Acre Wood | USA | Triumph TR-7 | Doug Shepherd |
| Olympus | USA | Triumph Tr-7 | Doug Shepherd |
| Susquehannock Trail | USA | Triumph TR-7 | Doug Shepherd |
| Baie des Chaleurs | Canada | Triumph TR-7 | Doug Shepherd |
| Chisum Trail | USA | Triumph TR-7 | Doug Shepherd |
| Northern Lites | USA | Triumph TR-7 | Doug Shepherd |
| Press On Regardless | USA | Triumph TR-7 | Doug Shepherd |

* SCCA PRO Rally National Champion
* SCCA/CASC North American Rally Cup Champion
* NARRA National Rally Champion

## 1979
| 100 Acre Wood | USA | Triumph TR-7 | Doug Shepherd |
| Chisum Trail | USA | Triumph TR-8 | Doug Shepherd |
| Piston les Wapitis | Canada | Triumph TR-8 | Doug Shepherd |
| La Jornada Trabajosa | USA | Triumph TR-7 | Fred Gallagher |
| Highlands Rally | Canada | Triumph TR-8 | Doug Shepherd |
| Happiness Is Sunrise | USA | Triumph TR-8 | Doug Shepherd |
| Northern Lites | USA | Triumph TR-8 | Doug Shepherd |

* SCCA PRO Rally National Champion

## 1980
| 100 Acre Wood | USA | Triumph TR-8 | Doug Shepherd |
| Tour De Forest | USA | Triumph TR-8 | Doug Shepherd |
| Northern Lites | USA | Triumph TR-8 | Doug Shepherd |
| Chisum Trail | USA | Triumph TR-8 | Doug Shepherd |
| Piston les Wapitis | Canada | Triumph TR-8 | Doug Shepherd |
| Baie des Chaleurs | Canada | Triumph TR-8 | Doug Shepherd |

| | | | |
|---|---|---|---|
| Highlands Rally | Canada | Triumph TR-8 | Fred Gallagher |
| Lobster Rally | Canada | Triumph TR-8 | Fred Gallagher |
| Happiness Is Sunrise | USA | Triumph TR-8 | Doug Shepherd |

* SCCA PRO Rally National Champion
* SCCA/CASC North American Rally Cup Champion

## 1981
| | | | |
|---|---|---|---|
| Big Bend Bash | USA | Peugeot 504 | Doug Shepherd |

## 1982
| | | | |
|---|---|---|---|
| Nor'Wester | USA | Audi Quattro | Doug Shepherd |
| Olympus | USA | Audi Quattro | Doug Shepherd |
| Northern Lites | USA | Audi Quattro | Doug Shepherd |
| Susquehannock Trail | USA | Audi Quattro | Doug Shepherd |
| Lobster Rally | Canada | Audi Quattro | Doug Shepherd |
| Sunriser Forest Rally | USA | Audi Quattro | Doug Shepherd |
| Centennial | USA | Audi Quattro | Doug Shepherd |
| Tour De Forest | USA | Audi Quattro | Sam Moses |
| Press On Regardless | USA | Audi Quattro | Doug Shepherd |
| SnoDrift | USA | Audi Quattro | Tom Grimshaw |

* SCCA PRO Rally National Champion
* Pikes Peak Auto Hillclimb Rally Class Champion
* AARWBA All-American Auto Racing Team

## 1983
| | | | |
|---|---|---|---|
| Sachs Winter Rally | Germany | Audi Quattro | Arwed Fischer |
| 100 Acre Wood Rally | USA | Audi Quattro | Doug Shepherd |
| Sunriser Forest Rally | USA | Audi Quattro | Doug Shepherd |
| Nor'Wester | USA | Audi Quattro | Doug Shepherd |
| Michigan International | USA | Audi Quattro | Neil Wilson |
| Susquehannock Trail | USA | Audi Quattro | Neil Wilson |
| Lobster Rally | Canada | Audi Quattro | Doug Shepherd |
| Highlands Rally | Canada | VW GTI | Linda Wilcox |
| Rocky Mountain | Canada | Audi Quattro | Doug Shepherd |
| Manistee Trail | USA | Audi Quattro | Doug Shepherd |
| Carson City International | USA | Audi Quattro | Doug Shepherd |

289

* SCCA PRO Rally National Champion
* SCCA/CASC North American Rally Cup Champion
* Pikes Peak Auto Hillclimb Rally Class Champion
* AARWBA All-American Auto Racing Team

## 1984

| | | | |
|---|---|---|---|
| Nor'Wester | USA | Audi Quattro | Harry Ward |
| Michigan International | USA | Audi Quattro | Fred Gallagher |
| Susquehannock Trail | USA | Audi Quattro | Neil Wilson |
| Lobster Rally | Canada | Audi Quattro | Paul Choiniere |
| Sunriser Forest Rally | USA | Audi Quattro | Neil Wilson |
| Cyprus Rally | Cyprus | Audi Quattro | Fred Gallagher |
| Dyfi Ste. Agathe | Canada | Audi Quattro | Tom Grimshaw |
| Oregon Trail | USA | Audi Quattro | Tom Grimshaw |

* SCCA PRO Rally National Champion
* SCCA/CASC North American Rally Cup Champion

## 1985

| | | | |
|---|---|---|---|
| Wild West Rally | USA | Audi Quattro | Tom Grimshaw |
| Dartmouth Highlands | Canada | Audi Quattro | Tom Grimshaw |
| Battle Creek Rally | USA | Audi Quattro | Tom Grimshaw |
| Dyfi Ste. Agathe | Canada | Audi Quattro | Tom Grimshaw |
| Sunriser Forest Rally | USA | Sport Quattro | Tom Grimshaw |
| Carson City International | USA | Sport Quattro | Tom Grimshaw |

* SCCA PRO Rally National Champion
* SCCA/CASC North American Rally Cup Champion

## 1986

| | | | |
|---|---|---|---|
| Perce Neige | Canada | Sport Quattro | Tom Grimshaw |
| Tulip 200 | USA | Sport Quattro | Tom Grimshaw |
| Nor'Wester | USA | Sport Quattro | Tom Grimshaw |
| Susquehannock Trail | USA | Sport Quattro | Tom Grimshaw |
| Arkansas Traveler | USA | Sport Quattro | Tom Grimshaw |

| | | | |
|---|---|---|---|
| Ojibwe Rally | USA | Sport Quattro | Tom Grimshaw |
| Dyfi Ste. Agathe | Canada | Audi Quattro | Tom Grimshaw |
| Press On Regardless | USA | Sport Quattro | Tom Grimshaw |

\* SCCA PRO Rally National Champion
\* SCCA/CASC North American Rally Cup Champion
\* World Record: National Championship Wins

## 1987

| | | | |
|---|---|---|---|
| Perce Neige | Canada | Audi Quattro | Paul Choiniere |
| Barbary Coast | USA | Sport Quattro | Tom Grimshaw |
| Centennial Rally | USA | Sport Quattro | Tom Grimshaw |
| Susquehannock Trail | USA | Sport Quattro | Tom Grimshaw |
| Sunriser Forest Rally | USA | Sport Quattro | Tom Grimshaw |
| Voyager Rally | Canada | Coupe Quattro | Paul Choiniere |
| Ojibwe Rally | USA | Sport Quattro | Tom Grimshaw |
| Dyfi Ste. Agathe | Canada | Sport Quattro | Tom Grimshaw |
| Press On Regardless | USA | Sport Quattro | Tom Grimshaw |
| Wild West | USA | Sport Quattro | Tom Grimshaw |
| Tall Pines | Canada | 4000S Quattro | Tom Grimshaw |

\* SCCA PRO Rally National Champion
\* SCCA/CASC North American Rally Cup Champion
\* AARWBA All-American Auto Racing Team
\* SCCA Robert V. Ridges Memorial Award

## 1988
| | | | |
|---|---|---|---|
| Perce Neige | Canada | 4000S Quattro | Tom Grimshaw |
| Baie des Chaleurs | Canada | Quattro Coupe | Trish Sparrow |

## 1990
| | | | |
|---|---|---|---|
| RAC | Canada | Quattro Coupe | Paul Choiniere |

SCCA: Sports Car Club of America, Inc.
CASC: Canadian Automobile Sport Clubs
NARA: North American Rally Association
NARRA: North American Rally Racing Association
AARWBA: American Auto Racing Writers & Broadcasters Assoc.

*"DNF: Did Not Finish." Sandy Liversidge, Saab 99, 1984 Michigan International PRO Rally. (Photo: Su Kemper)*

# Glossary

Many of the following terms are in common usage throughout the international world of rallying while others are intrinsic to North America. They are provided for the enlightenment of those not familiar with the sport of stage rallying.

BHP: Braking Horsepower

BOOKED IN: Checked into a timing control. On many stage rallies, teams carry a timing "book" which is presented for timing entries at each checkpoint.

BRACING PLACE: A metal plate mounted at an angle on the co-driver's side, allowing him to brace his feet and steady himself on a stage.

BULLBAG: An bag placed under a vehicle and inflated through a hose attached to the exhaust pipe—used as a car jack.

CHASE CAR: A team car that is not entered in the rally but stays in close contact with its competition car throughout the event, to gather helpful information and to provide emergency service and repairs.

CONTROL (or CHECKPOINT): A timing station.

COURSE CLOSING CAR: A vehicle that runs through a stage after all the competition cars, to alert spectators and marshals that the stage has been completed and will soon re-open for public travel.

COURSE OPENING CAR: A vehicle that runs through a stage just prior to the first competition car, to alert spectators and safety marshals that the stage is about to begin and to check that the stage road is properly set up and cleared for competition.

CRASH BOX: A gearbox that allows shifting without use of a clutch.

DNF/DNS: Did Not Finish/Did Not Start.

FACTORY TEAM: A team employed directly by an automobile manufacturer.

FIA: Federation Internationale de l'Automobile. Paris-based organi-

293

zation administering world motorsports.

FISA: Federation Internationale du Sport Automobile. A division of FIA.

FLAT (Right or Left): A pacenote term describing a road that goes essentially straight, but with a slight bend.

FORCE MAJEURE: Dictionary: a superior or irresistible force. A stage rally rule requiring teams to complete a stage once it has been declared open for competition, except in the case of medical emergency. The SCCA National PRO Rally Championship Rules state: While event organizers have an obligation, as far as is reasonable, to ensure every competitor shall encounter equal course conditions and equal likelihood of hazard, incidents often occur which are beyond the organizer's control. When a competitor encounters such a hazard and receives additional penalty time, it is bad luck. The obstruction is "Force Majeure."

4WD/4WS: Four-wheel-drive/Four-wheel-steering.

FREE LATENESS: Extra time allowance for competitors to arrive late at a checkpoint without penalty.

GROUP A: FIA international rally car classification that allows extensive modifications and which requires a minimum production of 2,500 for homologation. Group A is the dominant group in current world championship rallies.

GROUP N: FIA international rally car classification which allows very limited modifications to standard production vehicles. Similar to North America's Production Class.

GUMBO: A particularly nasty type of mud that is extremely slippery and dries to the consistency (and color) of concrete.

GYMKHANA: Dictionary—A meet featuring sports contests (such as racing). In the U.S., a sports car gymkhana features cars racing, one at a time, against the clock, through a course usually outlined by pylons in a large paved area.

HIGH CENTERED: Stuck–with the wheels off the ground.

MARQUE: Dictionary—A brand or make of a product (such as a

sports car).

M&S: A tire tread designed to handle mud and snow.

ONE-OFF: A special built one-of-a-kind vehicle.

OPENS: A term applied when the severity of a curve decreases.

OVERSTEER: A cornering characteristic that occurs when the rear wheels lose traction and begin to slide out before the front wheels. The opposite of understeer.

PACENOTES: A series of shorthand style notes, prepared by a rally team during practice before start of the event, describing in detail the severity of curves and turns on a stage road. Pacenotes are read continuously to the driver by the co-driver during stage competition. Example: FR/C 30 HPL + MR> . . . Interpretation: Fast right over crest, (30 meters to next note), hairpin left and medium right, tightens . . .

PARC EXPOSE: A parking area open to competitors and public, used for public viewing of rally cars. Maintenance and repairs are allowed.

PARC FERME: A closed parking area where competitor and service crew access is not allowed. No vehicle servicing is allowed.

PERFORMANCE RALLY: Endurance. An event based on high speed driving and vehicle/team

PRESS STAGE: Usually a short section of closed road set up before an event to give demo rides and provide photo opportunities for the media.

RALLYMASTER: In early years, the organizer of a rally. Today the term has been modernized to: "Event Chairman," "Event Organizer," or the like.

RALLYSPRINT: A short rally course (usually a single stage), often run several times by each team in an elimination format.

ROAD PENALTY: Early or late arrival timing penalty taken on a transit during a stage rally. Transits, on open roads between closed stages, are called "road sections."

REST  HALT: A period of time during which competition is temporarily stopped. Rest halts can range from a short thirty minute break to a two hour dinner halt, or a full over night halt.

SECRET RALLY: A stage rally that does not allow practice or pacenoting before the start. All North American national and divisional stage rallies are secret. All world championship rallies are pacenote rallies and allow practice.

SEEDING: A method of rating drivers based on past performance. The highest international seed group is FIA Priority A. The highest SCCA National PRO Rally seed group in the U.S. is FIA Seed, followed by Seeds 1 through 6. The highest seeded drivers start before lower seeded drivers.

SERVICE CREW: A team of mechanics who perform maintenance and repairs on the rally car during competition.

SLICKS: A tire with an essentially smooth tread used primarily on paved surfaces.

SOLO:  A modern day form of gymkhana.

SPEED OBSERVATION CONTROL: Commonly called an "0 Control" in North America. A secret checkpoint placed on a transit to record speeds of rally cars to assure they do not exceed legal limits. SPIKED (OR STUDDED) TIRES: Metal spikes mounted in the tire tread for added traction on ice and snow. In addition to small carborundum- tipped  steel spikes, several other innovations were tried in the U.S. "Shredded Wheat" and "Walnuts" were thousands of tiny steel wires or broken walnut shells moulded into the tread.

SPECTATOR STAGE: A rally stage road containing pre-set spectator points announced to the public and controlled by safety marshals.

STAY IN IT: Keep the power on.

STUFFED: Falling, spinning, driving, rolling and/or crashing off the road.

SWEEP CAR: A vehicle, traveling behind the course closing car, equipped to assist in the removal of disabled rally cars on a stage road.

TEE: A junction where the travelled road ends at another road forming a "T" configuration and requiring a turn left or right. It is not possible to go straight at a "Tee."

TIGHTENS: A term applied when the severity of a curve increases.

TIME BAR: The amount of accumulated lateness or earliness time, usually expressed in minutes, which, if exceeded, bars a team from further competition. In North America time bar is usually ten minutes early and thirty minutes late for a major section of an event.

TULIP DRAWING: (Also called an Alpine Drawing). A route book diagram depicting the correct route at each instructed intersection. The term originated from the Tulip Rally in Holland many years ago.

WARNING TRIANGLE: A reflective triangular shaped warning device, approved by the U.S. Department of Transportation—set on the road to warn that a car has stopped on the course. In the U.S. stage rally cars are required to carry a minimum of three warning triangles.

WCR: World Championship Rally.

WORKS TEAM: The same as a Factory Team.

WRC: World Rally Championships.

# Bibliography

Anderson, Eric, *Performance Rallying*. New York: Sports Car Press, 1975.

Buhlmann, Klaus, *Kimberley's Rally Team Guide No. 1—Audi*. London, England: Menoshire Ltd., 1984.

Byrne, Robert, *1,911 Best Things Anybody Ever Said*, New York: Ballantine Books, 1988.

Goss, Clint, *The Road Rally Handbook*. Westport, Conn.: Rally America Publishing, 1993.

Holmes, Martin, *Rally Navigation*. Somerset, England:Haynes Publishing Group, 1983.

Holmes Martin and Hugh Bishop, *Rothmans World Rallying 2*.London, England: Osprey Publishing Limited, 1980.

Lamm, Jam, *All Wheel Drive High Performance Handbook*. Osceola, Wisc.: Motorbooks International, 1990.

Wooldridge, Richard, *International Rally Sport 1979/80*. Abingdon, Oxfordshire, England: S & S Press, 1979.

Vatanen, Ari (with Vesa Vaisanen*). Every Second Counts*, Harrow Midds, England: SAF Publishing Ltd., 1985.

## PERIODICALS

*Sports Car*, Sports Car Club of America, Inc., 9033 East Easter Place, Englewood, CO 80112.

*Sports Illustrated*, 1271 Avenue of the Americas, New York, NY 10020.

*Car and Driver*, 2002 Hogback Rd., Ann Arbor, MI 48105.

*Motor Trend*, 8490 Sunset Blvd., Los Angeles, CA 90069.

*Road & Track*, 1499 Monrovia Ave., Newport Beach, CA 92663

*Dusty Times*, Hillside Racing Corporation, 20751 Marilia St., Chatsworth, CA 91311.

*Rally Magazine*, 706 Roxbury Road, Southbury, CT 06488.

*AutoWeek Magazine*, 1400 Woodbridge, Detroit, MI 48207.

*Rally Sport Magazine*, 59 Murdock Rd., Oxon, Bicester, Bicester, England

*AutoSport* Magazine

Pikes Peak Hillclimb Association

# About the Author

TOM GRIMSHAW was born 1933 in Detroit, Michigan and spent most of his working life as a financial controller for several large corporations. He discovered the sport of rallying when a friend took him on a small club event in 1958— it was also his first experience with the term "DNF" (Did Not Finish).

His first sports car was a 1961 Triumph TR-3 which he drove on several club rallies until finances forced him to begin accepting rides in the navigator's seat. He soon realized he was a far better navigator than driver.

Tom's first taste of high speed rallying was on the Canadian Winter Rallies and the Trans-Canada Shell 4000s. In 1965 he and his driver, Gerhardt Rasche, were hired by Scott Harvey to drive a Simca 1000 for the Chrysler National Rally Team. On their third event they rolled the Simca end-over-end several times, landed on their wheels, and pushed on to place 15th overall out of a starting field of 140 cars, and first in their class.

Since those early days, Tom has co-driven (navigated) for many factory-sponsored rally teams until finally joining John Buffum in the Audi Quattro in 1985. During each of their three years together, Buffum and Grimshaw won the SCCA National PRO Rally Championships and the combined U.S./Canada North American Rally Cup Championships.

In addition to his stage rally successes, Tom has also won The Alcan 5000 Rally (Audi) and six One Lap of America Rallies (Audi, Dodge, Toyota, BMW).

Throughout his rally career Tom has contributed articles to many motor sport publications and received an award for the best monthly column of the year from the SCCA's *Sports Car* magazine.

Tom is single and lives on the Gulf Coast of Florida.

301